Trade-In Arbitrage

The system for getting paid to search Amazon for hidden gold, and know your profits before you spend a penny

Trade-In Arbitrage: The system for getting paid to search Amazon for hidden gold, and know your profits before you spend a penny

All rights reserved. No part of this book or site may be reproduced or redistributed in any form or by any electronic or mechanical means, including information storage and retrieval systems, without permission in writing from the author and publisher, except by a reviewer who may quote brief passages in a review.

Copyright © 2019 Peter Valley

www.FBAmastery.com

peter@fbamastery.com

The story of how I got into Amazon trade-in arbitrage is really weird.

This book only happened through a strange combination of hacking, peer pressure, and revenge. Let me back up...

About two and a half years ago, I announced to the readers of my site FBAmastery.com that I was doing a free webinar called "*Online Book Arbitrage*." The webinar had nothing to do with trade-in credit arbitrage (and I'm barely going to talk about old-fashioned "online book arbitrage" in this book), but I really wanted the webinar to be worth people's time. I had never done a webinar before, and I *really* wanted to over-deliver. So I was trying to think of some cool bonus tricks I could share at the end related to sourcing on Amazon, and then reselling back on Amazon.

I thought of one trick I'd been doing casually for about a year, involving Amazon's trade-in store. Even though the trick wasn't directly related to the subject of the webinar, it was still a cool free trick people would get value from.

It went like this: Install a browser extension called "Context Search," go to Amazon's trade-in store, then highlight and right-click the ISBNs and run those ISBNs as a search through BookFinder.com. That will bring up the cheapest copy of that book on the internet. Anytime you find a book for sales cheaper than Amazon's trade-in, you get to profit the difference (in trade-in credit). Then you can roll that credit into even more credit, and get a snowball effect until you're ready to cash out.

And what's better, once you're ready to cash out, you can invest that credit into books you can sell for an even greater cash amount (we'll outline this formula at the end, but this process is covered in more detail in my prequel to the book you're reading, titled *Online Book Arbitrage*, available free at www.OnlineBookArbitrage.com).

This means you can literally take $100 and turn it into $1,000 (or more), by trading credit into more credit, and then cashing out for actual cash.

So I dedicated about 90 seconds to this trick on my webinar. Truth was, I had only done this trick myself every now and then. It took a lot of time, and I had always preferred dealing 100% in cash, even if the credit was essentially "free."

Fast forward about a year

Out of nowhere, there was a buzz in the Amazon selling world: Amazon trade-in credit "arbitrage" was the new gold rush. I had no idea where it was coming from, but the buzz was deafening.

I have some suspicions that whoever was promoting this concept was on my webinar that day (as far as I know I was the first to talk about trade-in arbitrage publicly), but beyond this I have no reason to think I had anything to do with this sudden trend.

The concept of profiting off trade-in was very enticing. To recap, it went like this:

There are hundreds of thousands of books (and around half a million items total) that Amazon will offer instant trade-in credit for.

If you find a copy (book, CD, video game, etc) for sale on literally any site in the world that costs *less* than the trade-in value, you get to profit the difference (in Amazon trade-in credit, which can be traded up to cash, as we'll discuss).

And not "profit" in the speculative sense the way you're used to if you already sell on Amazon: Amazon actually locks in the trade-in amount, and as soon as the item is shipped and received, you receive the credit. (Almost) zero risk.

No more wondering about prices dropping, dealing with seller feedback, repricing, or virtually any headaches we're used to dealing with selling products on Amazon.

It appeals to the secret (or not so secret) lazy person in all of us: Get paid (credit) to click around the internet, and the outcome is guaranteed (only marginal risk – Amazon locks in that price and guarantees it for 21 days).

Where was the "trade-in" hype coming from?

Like I said, my inbox was increasingly filling up with questions about my thoughts on "Amazon trade-in arbitrage." So I started to ask people: Why are you asking? Where is this all coming from?

From what I heard, the #1 instigator seemed to be a program called "Textbook Money" (rumored to have since changed their name to "Book Trades Biz.") The information I was gathering indicated they were promoting a high-priced browser extension that embedded trade-in values on the Amazon page, and alerted you if there were items cheaper than their trade-in value.

I also gathered that "Textbook Money" had generated so much buzz in such a short amount of time using a simple model: Partner with people who have a large online presence and a large email list, get them to promote a free webinar, pitch a product on the webinar, then share the profits with the promoter. From what I could tell, "Textbook Money" had partnered with at least 15 internet marketers with large email lists, and carpet-bombed the internet with promotions.

This had nothing to do with me and little to do with anything I taught, so why do I care?

There was a very dark side to the "trade-in" trend

This is the part I haven't mentioned yet. That initial tidal wave of emails I received came from the first wave of Textbook Money users. And they were in a complete panic. They had paid $997 + $97 a month for this crude browser extension, and realized they'd been scammed. Not only were they not making their money back, they weren't even close.

Email after email came in from people who had fallen for the Textbook Money sales pitch, which promised (among other things) $500,000 a year in profits using their system. The users were completely freaking out, having sometimes sunk their life savings into something that didn't work.

(I have an article on FBAmastery.com with screenshots of over 50 of these emails from panicked and angry ex-members).

From my personal experience, I knew the numbers and knew the level of opportunity. It was out there. But any tool that facilitated the hunt for trade-in opportunity was not worth an upfront cost of $1,000.

Still, I didn't have any skin in this game so it was nothing more to me than another unfortunate case of internet hucksters promoting the latest internet scam.

Then it got weirder

I started to get even more emails. The second round went like this:

"Hey Peter, did you hear Textbook Money copied you?"

I quickly learned it was true. To expand their "get rich quick" empire, Textbook Money had made a direct clone of my tool, Zen Arbitrage. While Zen Arbitrage didn't directly relate to trade-in, it was a good supplement to trade-in arbitrage tactics, allowing you to roll trade-in credit into books that could be sold for cash. In other words, it was the missing link in any credit-to-cash system.

Since Zen Arbitrage started to get so many of their former customers, the Textbook Money hucksters decided just to copy us and charge almost 3x as much.

I got a look at their Zen Arbitrage clone, and it was terrible, slow, and barely functioned. But it was a knock-off, no question.

So, that was weird.

Then it got even weirder

A lot weirder.

Around this time, the lead developer at Zen Arbitrage noticed some unusual activity among users. One of our subscribers was logging a highly unusual number of searches in our book database.

It was quickly determined the activity was the work not of a human, but a "screen scraping" bot. These bots are created by hackers to mimic human behavior, including "clicking" and "scrolling" behind website paywalls to steal data.

It was clear this unusual activity was the work of a bot that was stealing our data.

What were the hackers after?

The theory was simple: Our data. There's money in data, and Zen Arbitrage has the best. Specifically, info collected on over 22 million books.

Also in our database is data no one else has, including six month average sales rank, a textbook-only database, another database containing thousands of books with book arbitrage / resale value, and more.

The timing of the hack (or its second wave, as I'll explain) coincided with a massive overhaul of our database and data harvesting. To put it simply, we expanded our database and the rate at which we refresh the data, making our already exceptional database even more appetizing to hackers.

If your online arbitrage database is complete garbage, you'll definitely want to copy, infiltrate, or otherwise beat down the door of Zen Arbitrage. *(Another bad knockoff called "Eflip" later did the same thing.)*

What does this have to do with Textbook Money? Just wait...

The counter-attack

Our lead developer is 3 parts genius and 1 part prankster, so rather than block bots, he does something even better: Feeds them a mountain of garbage data.

While the bot was requesting data about books on Amazon such as ISBNs, average sales rank, and trade-in value, what they got was completely useless but appeared accurate: Books with incorrect values, inaccurate ISBNs, and totally fake trade-in value.

"Hackers get hacked." That's our motto.

The hackers expose themselves

After a few months of that, the thieves made two fatal mistakes.

First, they tripled their requests. This caused page load time for Zen Arbitrage to slow, triggered alarms behind the scenes, and provoked us to investigate.

Second, they pulled a move so amateur, its defies belief: They hammered us with request from an easily traceable IP address.

It was the IP for "Textbook Money":

"52.87.121.99" is the IP where the Textbook Money app is hosted (their app, as distinct from their sales page URL):

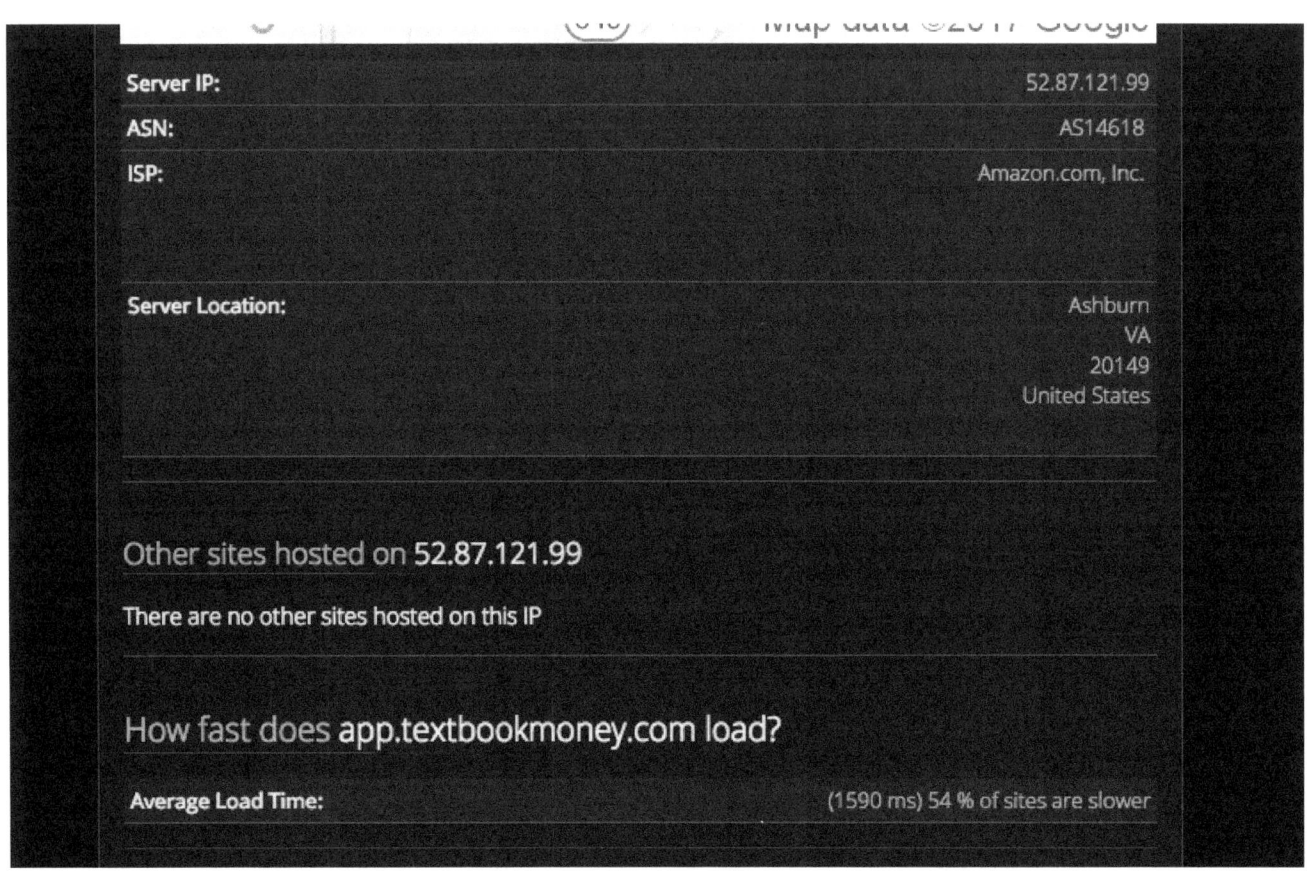

Note: "There are no other sites hosted on this IP."

The prank thickens

For months, we'd been feeding the mystery thieves mountains of garbage data. Completely inaccurate gibberish.

If a book had a rank of 100,000, we fed the attackers a rank of 3 million. If it had a trade-in value of $2.31, we said it was $110. We scrambled ISBNs, titles, everything.

Anyone trying to use this data to make money with online book arbitrage would be instantly out of business. It was unusable.

The plot thickened when we figured out the infiltrators were Textbook Money

This is where it got interesting.

In analyzing their motive, our only reasonable assumption was:

"Textbook Money is stealing our data, and selling it to their customers."

Remember, the data they were getting (and selling?) was complete garbage.

That means any customers they may have sold our data to were getting…. complete garbage.

Do you see how poetic this justice is? (Justice for the culprits, not their unwitting subscribers)

If the theory was true, Textbook Money has been selling their customers completely inaccurate garbage for months

Any data they stole from us and then sold to their customers was completely garbage, and their customers were getting sold complete garbage.

And if accurate, Textbook Money reselling the garbage data we'd been feeding them would explain the huge up-tick in bad reviews, angry customers, and exodus out of Textbook Money (and over to Zen Arbitrage) around the time we started sending them garbage data.

This might be the most poetic justice in the history of poetic justice.

The wheels of justice start to turn

In the midst of sorting out how much data the culprits had stole from us, we got a look at the actual Textbook Money Chrome extension. What does a $1,000 + $97/month piece of software look like?

It was kind of staggering. As in, staggeringly bad. Staggering simplistic. Staggeringly unimpressive.

The trade-in data was incomplete. The profit estimation figures were completely insane. And the links were weird. Why would you link to Craigslist in an online arbitrage tool?

Our developer said: "They charge $1,000 for this? This unbelievably simple. It would be really easy to make this, and make it better."

Next step: Become an expert in the trade-in and buyback game

Once my developer got to work, I had my own work to do.

I set out to learn everything I could about the trade-in & book buy back sites. I wasn't going to promote anything I wasn't 100% enthusiastic about. And it goes without saying I wasn't going to promote a business model that simply didn't work.

I began to get intimate with Amazon trade-in data. Over at Zen Arbitrage (again, not a trade-in tool exactly), we've built a massive data harvesting system that is processing tens of millions of products daily. Buried among this, was trade-in value not just for books, but everything. As far as the trade-in data, I never really paid attention to it. But after the buzz over Amazon trade-in became a deafening roar, I started to look at the data more closely.

With access to this data, I know exactly what the numbers look like. Exactly what the opportunity is, the price fluctuations, and more. Over the next few months, I got to know the numbers intimately.

From looking at this numbers, I can give a more sober take on exactly what the opportunities are in trade-in credit arbitrage (fancy term for buying low and instantly selling high).

What I learned was encouraging, even as an old-school bookseller. I learned things like:

- Just how often prices on Amazon actually drop below their trade-in value (its not insanely common, but it happens a lot more than I thought).
- The existence of book buy back sites (I barely knew these existed before, but I learned they will often pay more in cash than a book costs on Amazon, and they lock in a price – you don't even have to wait for a sale.)
- How often book buy back sites will pay more in cash than you can buy it for on Amazon (This is where it gets even better: Instant cash opportunity, and skipping trade-in altogether. This happens WAY more than I thought.)
- Using trade-in values to detect severely underpriced offers on Amazon (so you can skip trade-in altogether, identify underpriced books, and make quick cash sales on Amazon for a profit.)

After digging into the data and spending months practicing it myself, I soon knew two things:

1. This was a legitimate and profitable business model.
2. The people teaching this material already didn't realize its full potential. Yes, they were charging $1,000 for it, but the part they didn't see was the cash potential: Such as mining the trade-in store for cash buy back sites, "price proximity," and how to convert credit to cash — all of which we'll get into.

Why did I write this book?

Yes, if you're wondering, it was partly inspired by a karmic desire to give away for free what Textbook Money is charging $1,000 for (they really hype up their training, which I hear isn't as good as what I'm giving away in this book).

The other motivation is the inspiration I've received from talking to so many Amazon sellers over the years who drop out and quit the business, then asking them *why* they quit the business.

Almost every reason falls under the umbrella of "uncertainty." Sources drying up, prices dropping, inventory not selling. When you talk to Amazon sellers, all the big reasons they're unhappy are really one reason: An aversion to uncertainty.

In writing this book, I wanted to introduce a model that worked for sellers who want a business with minimal uncertainty — where you know your profits before you spend a penny.

So that's the story of this book

I've been teaching Amazon selling for a few years, done bunch of books and courses, and everything I've taught has been motivated first and foremost by my own experiences as an Amazon seller. While I had toyed with trade-in arbitrage for a couple years, this is the first model I've taught that I was mostly forced to learn by sleazy internet marketers (and the choir of "popular demand" i.e. requests for this material.)

But I'm glad I did. So here it is: A system for surfing Amazon, finding items cheaper than their trade-in or buy back site value, and profiting the difference.

-Peter Valley

peter@fbamastery.com

Here's my promise with this book:

I've felt cheated in the past when I've downloaded an ebook only to find out I needed to buy a bunch of tools or something to apply the material. So there was no way I was going to write an ebook (especially a free one) that makes you pay for a bunch of things to use it. So here's the standard I set throughout this book:

Nothing I'm writing about requires any paid tools whatsoever, and I've deliberately avoided mentioning any tools that cost money.

In fact, I was so strict, I left out really obviously helpful tools simply because they cost money. I was committed to keeping this a "poor man's system," where the only cost was the variable expense of inventory.

If you finish this book and want to take this to the next level, email me at peter@fbamastery.com and I'll refer you to a few paid tools that streamline this process.

Who Is Trade-In Arbitrage For?

Quick note before we proceed: How do you know if this is a business model for you?

The trade-in game almost seems too good to be true. Is there such a thing as easy, risk-free money on the internet?

Yes and no.

"Yes," if you avoid the most basic mistakes, the risks are minimal (basically a shady seller sending an incorrect/damaged book).

"No," in that it's not as easy as some "get rich quick" hucksters make you think.

I really dislike the "ger rich quick" people, and almost all "make money online" hype. Either they mislead you about the level of opportunity, or overstate how easy it is to find it. So let's get totally clear and repeat after me (or at least read the next two lines):

1. This system takes work.
2. You won't find opportunity on every page (or 3 pages).

The people who do well at trade-in credit arbitrage are willing to dedicate serious time to scouring the Amazon trade-in store, and hunting opportunity across the internet like a laser-focused predator.

They accept the trade-off: In exchange for the elegance and simplicity of near-risk-free, totally online sourcing, they're willing to dedicate significant time to hunting down the profit.

(If you're one of those people with a short attention span who tends to give up if you don't achieve results in 5 minutes, don't even try this. It does work, but its not that simple.)

I never like getting halfway through a book before realizing the material isn't a fit for me, so let's get this out upfront...

This book is not for you if:

1. You must have instant results, and need money to just comes out of your computer in 5 minutes or less.
2. You can't stand sitting at a computer for more than a few minutes.

This isn't a system that produces results on every single page in Amazon. In fact, this won't even work on 1/50 items. Like all good (non-criminal) things, this takes work.

This book is for you if:

1. You're willing to trade spending more time to hunt for opportunity for running a low-risk business totally from your computer.
2. You don't like risk.

3. You want to know your profits before you invest a penny.

There are many types of online entrepreneurs. Those who love risk, and those who are terrified of it. Those who love steady repetition, and those who can't stand it. Those who like complexity, and those who want the simplest and most streamlined system possible.

If all that sounds good, let's get into it...

Understanding Amazon's Trade-In Program

Keep in mind before we proceed: The system we're outlining in this book works as well if not better for cash buy back sites outside of Amazon, and we'll get to those in a minute. But this system is always about getting cash in the end, and the goal with Amazon trade-credit is always to convert to cash.

So even when we're talking about Amazon credit, we're really talking about cash.

What is Amazon's trade-in program?

Within Amazon is a separate "store" of sorts, only instead of taking your money, they *give* you money (in the form of Amazon store credit). Depending on the season, Amazon's trade-in store can have over half a million products that Amazon will accept for trade-in credit.

Click a button, print a (free) shipping label, ship them the product, and the trade-in amount is credited to your account within days.

It's a common myth that Amazon offers trade-in value for everything they sell. In fact, its only the most high-demand items. The amounts to a very small percentage of their entire catalog (well under 1%). For example, in the books category, depending on the season, there is about 250,000 listings in the trade-in store. The total number of books on Amazon is over 25 million, which makes the trade-in offers less than 1% of their total books catalog.

(We'll get to book buy back sites in the next chapter. These are actually very similar, but better.)

How Amazon's Trade-In Store Works

To submit a trade-in:

- Go to the Trade-In Store and search for eligible items
- Click "Trade-In" to submit the item for trade-in.
- Select the condition of your item(s) based on the criteria listed, then click Continue.
- Click "Submit" to submit your trade-in and print your prepaid UPS shipping label.
- Ship your items within 21 days.

A Few Facts About Amazon's Trade-In Program

The price is locked in for 21 days: As long as the book is shipped by then, you're guaranteed this amount. To those whose biggest frustration about selling on Amazon is price volatility, you'll love this.

Amazon pays for shipping: They issue you a pre-paid shipping label, so just get it to UPS and the rest is taken care of.

Amazon only offers trade-in value for high-demand books: Their whole business model here is offering a smaller amount than they expect to sell this for, and only for high-demand books. In the Books category, it is rare to see something ranked worse than 500,000, and most books are better than 100,000 (i.e. high demand).

The trade-in value is inherently a fraction of its expected sales price: The higher the demand for the book, the higher the percentage of its average sales price Amazon will offer in trade-in value, but naturally the trade-in value is always less than Amazon expects to sell it for. Buy low, sell high. Amazon is just doing a smarter version of what we're doing already.

Downsides To Trade-in Credit Arbitrage

Anytime an internet marketer touts "Make instant internet profits with no risk and without leaving your computer!!!" get very suspicious. They're leaving something out.

Guys like Luke Lambo and "Textbook Money" have spread a lot of hype (and made a lot of enemies) over trade-in credit arbitrage, so let me give a more sober take.

Here's the *other* side of trade-in credit arbitrage:

- It's hard.
- It's volatile.
- You're inherently not getting the full value for your items.

It's hard: By hard, I don't mean "digging ditches" hard. You are in your pajamas on your computer, after all. You have to spend a lot of time scouring Amazon and Bookfinder.com links to make serious trade credit. There are tools that will streamline this, but it is not "fast, easy, and instant results."

It's volatile: I've seen the numbers. When there is a product on Amazon whose price drops below the trade-in price, it is usually gone in under a couple hours.

You're not getting the full value for your books: By the nature of the fact Amazon is offering "X" for a book, that book has a cash market value of more than "X." Amazon will always pay you in trade less than what they can sell it for. That means you can always get more selling that book for cash, and you're forfeiting that option in exchange for instant profits and not having to wait for a sale.

Why do trade-in credit at all? Why not just sell the book for cash? You absolutely can. In fact I encourage it.

But for the sake of this book, I'm going to assume you're the type of person trade-in & buy back arbitrage appeals to: A certain type of risk-averse seller who doesn't want to deal with volatility – you want something guaranteed.

Upsides to Trade-in Credit Arbitrage

- The prices are locked in: You no longer have to worry about price fluctuations and dropping prices.
- You don't have to wait for a sale: Once Amazon or the cash buy back site receives the book, payment is instant.
- Shipping is free – Amazon and most buy back sites pay for it: Just print a shipping label and you're good to go.

- You don't have to leave your computer.

Amazon Trade-in Credit – By The Numbers

Here's the total number of offers in each category of Amazon's trade-in store (on average, it fluctuates wildly):

   Books: 125,000 to 400,000
   Music: 125,000
   DVDs: 100,000
   Video games: 10,000

Total in Amazon's trade-in store right now: 500,000 (approxiate)

That's the trade-in program in a nutshell.

Profiting Off Book Buy Back Sites

This is where it gets even better.

I was completely in the dark about book buy back sites until somewhat recently. I had seen the "BookScouter" link (similar BookFinder.com/buyback, which scans the top cash buy back sites) inside my book sourcing scanning app (which I use for my offline sourcing), and had the same assumption as I had about Amazon trade-in: The buy back site value is always going to be less than the cash value of selling the book on Amazon, so why would I send it to a cash buy back site when I could just sell it for more?

It felt like the lazy-man's way to insure you didn't get the full value of your books. So I ignored book buy back sites. But I was wrong in some key ways.

What are book buy back sites?

Simply put, these are sites that pay a fixed price for books listed on their site - in cash. Basically it works just like Amazon's trade-in store, except you get cash (usually paid via PayPal).

Its interesting to observe the huge disparity cash buy back sites offers for individual books. One site will be offering $7 for a book, another will be offering $70. Don't ask me how this happens. I think each site has their own specific clients they serve (whether its certain schools, or who knows what) and this can cause huge demand for a book on one site where the demand is low on the others.

How are buy back sites like Amazon trade-in, and how are they different?

If you like Amazon trade-in, you'll *love* buy back sites. Just like Amazon's trade-in program, book buy back programs lock in a price, guarantee it for a set number of days, then pay you in cash.

As with Amazon's trade-in store, the buy back amount is usually going to be less than what you can get for the book by selling it on Amazon. But there's no wait, no listing, just instant profit.

Few facts about book buyback sites:

- There are over 35 of them.
- They lock in the price and (most) pay in cash.
- There is huge variation in how they pay, conditions standards, etc.
- They often pay more in cash than Amazon will in credit.

The last one is interesting.

Cash buy back values don't appear to be related to Amazon trade-in values whatsoever. In other words, there's no rule of thumb that goes "on average, cash buy back site offers are X% lower than Amazon's trade-in offer." Like I said, they have their own customer base and their own pricing algorithm. You would think market forces would apply uniformly across the entire book market, and cash buy back values would roughly be at pace with trade-in values (just a little bit less, since it is cash not credit, after all). Yet this is definitely not the case.

It's not uncommon to see books Amazon is offering $50 in credit for, that a cash buy back site is offering $100 for. Don't fight it, don't try to understand it, just enjoy it.

How do you submit to a buy back site?

Here's where I'm going to tactfully evade answering this question thoroughly, otherwise we'll be here all day. There are over 30 sites, with 30 different answers.

In addition to the submission process, here are some of the ways buy back sites differ among themselves:

- Shipping cost (free or not)
- Payment method
- Due date (when the book has to arrive)
- Minimums
- Condition standards

All this means that when submitting a book to a buy back site, there's an extra step in that you have to acquaint yourself with that particular site, their standards, and their submission process.

Where do you find book buyback site offers?

The best sources are:

- BookScouter.com
- BookFinder.com/buyback

These are basically the same.

Enter an ISBN into either, and they scan over 30 different book buyback sites, and show you the highest offer.

And in an upcoming chapter, I'm going to share a trick that allows us to scan every buy back site directly from Amazon with one click.

Here is the biggest and coolest fact about cash buy back sites

It is more common to find items below their cash buy back site value than their Amazon trade-in value.

That means that using the system we're outlining here, there is more profit to be made from cash buy back sites than Amazon trade-in.

This is the part the conversation about trade-in arbitrage misses, and is one of the main points of this book: Cash buy back sites are a huge part of this game.

Yes this book is called "Trade-In Arbitrage," but that's pure marketing. "Trade-In & Buy Back Site Arbitrage" just doesn't have a good ring.

How To Profit Off Amazon Trade-In Credit Arbitrage: A System Overview

How does one find trade-in opportunity?

Four ways:

1. Amazon to Amazon trades.
2. BookFinder to Amazon trades.
3. Amazon to book buy back site.
4. Bookfinder to book buy back site.

(There's a 5th tactic called the "underpriced book hack" that we'll get to in a later chapter. It's a little different, so its getting its own chapter).

Before we go into more detail, here's the basic trade-in credit mining formula we're going to outline in an upcoming chapter:

1. Search Amazon's trade-in store.
2. Assess if current lowest price for an item is lower than the Amazon trade-in value (yes this actually happens, as I'll cover in a moment).
3. Look up the highest cash buy back site value.
4. Run book through a book price comparison tool to find the cheapest copy anyone on the internet. Find copies cheaper than the trade-in or cash buy back site value.
5. Order the book.
6. Lock in the price, ship in the book, and get paid.

Now, let's break down the four ways to profit...

Profit method #1: Amazon-to-Amazon Trades

Is it possible to actually buy a book on Amazon for less than the trade-in value? And why would that even be possible?

Yes, you can do this. At any given moment, there are thousands of products on Amazon whose prices have fallen below the trade-in value (I'll give you some specific numbers in a second).

This means (almost) risk-free Amazon spending money – without even leaving Amazon.

This seems too good to be true, so how does this happen?

To illustrate how and why, let's take the Books category. On average there are 250,000 books in Amazon's trade-in store (give or take) at any given time. That's 250,000 opportunities for price anomalies, 250,000 products in constant price fluctuation, and 250,000 opportunities for the selling price to temporarily drop below the trade-in value. Prices for products are fluctuating like crazy all the time, usually multiple times a day, so there's nothing surprising about this.

Then consider that trade-in books are inherently high-demand. The average trade-in book is selling multiple copies daily. Let's just pick a lowball average figure and say the average across the trade-in store is 5 copies sold per day. (No one knows what the average is, but this feels like a safe number).

So we know that the price is changing at least 5 times a day (barring sales coming from a seller with multiple copies for sale). With copies so rapidly getting listed, sold, and repriced, this creates incredible price volatility (again, dramatically more than Amazon as a whole).

With these numbers, this means that to one degree or another, there are over one million price changes and one million small opportunities for the price to drop below the trade value. And that's just within the books category.

(I realize this is extremely flawed math, and I'm not trying give serious estimates here, just a general sense of price volatility).

And this doesn't even factor in new listings at weird prices, repricers doing the weird things they do often multiple times a day, and sellers manually pricing like crazy people and under-pricing the trade-in value.

All of this comes down to one thing: There are 1+ million price fluctuations daily within the Amazon book trade-in store, and over a million small potential opportunities for prices to drop below the trade-in value.

How often does this happen? I have specific numbers for you

How often does the lowest price on Amazon actually drop below the Amazon trade-in value?

We have a monster data-harvesting machine working 24-7 over at my online book arbitrage tool Zen Arbitrage. Although trade-in is not the primary function of Zen Arbitrage, we do store that data. So I have some "insider" numbers for you.

I just checked a moment before writing this, and looked at just at the figures for Books and DVDs (excluding all other categories). I have some real-time numbers.

At this moment there are 1,257 products you can purchase for prices below their trade-in value.

That's over 1,000 instant trade-in arbitrage opportunities, without leaving Amazon, in just two categories, at this moment.

Again, that's just at this moment (we don't store the numbers that would indicate how much lower or higher than average this "1,257" figure is on a given day).

Consider also that these opportunities come and go extremely fast. On any given day, its totally possible there are 10,000+ products appearing (and quickly disappearing) that can be bought and instantly traded in for a profit – all within Amazon.

And then consider I just looked at two categories (the only two we store data on right now). Across the entire Amazon trade-in store, this figure is certainly much higher.

What do these numbers translate to in terms of a percentage? How often will you see opportunities like this if you were just cruising around Amazon's trade-in store?

Right now there are 140,000 books in Amazon's trade-in store, and 80,000 DVDs. The figure fluctuates a lot, and 140,000 for books is unusually low.

For Books & DVDs, when you add 140,000 + 80,000, then divide by 1,257, it basically means this:

Approximately 1 out of every 175 products has a price lower than its trade-in value.

That's 1 in every 9.75 pages.

That's not cause for a complete lottery-winner freak out, but pretty incredible.

Quite a weird (and cool) glitch in the Amazon Matrix.

Profit method #2: Bookfinder-to-Amazon-trades

This is where it gets much easier.

Amazon prices tend to stay pretty stable relative to their trade-in value (174 out of 175 times, as we just established). But there are dozens of other bookselling sites across the internet. This is where it becomes a complete wildcard. Prices on other sites can be all over the place, and vary wildly.

A book can be $100 on Amazon, $70 on Powells, and $60 on eBay. Like I said, its just a complete wildcard.

So if you take any book with trade-in value and run it through these other sites, there's a significant chance of finding a copy not just cheaper than Amazon, but cheaper than its trade-in value.

Hopefully this is getting exciting for you.

To make this easier, the way we can do this with one click is BookFinder.com: BF scans over 40 bookselling sites, and sorts them lowest price to highest.

It is true that Amazon is the lowest price *most* of the time. But recent Amazon fees have made the potential for trade-in arbitrage using Bookfinder.com a lot more interesting…

Prior to the recent Amazon fees for books, I would estimate that Amazon had the lowest priced book of any site on the internet about 90% of the time (just an estimate).

After the new fees, selling books on other sites became a lot more interesting to a lot of sellers, and based on my unscientific observations, Amazon is now the lowest price copy on the internet a lot less. I would estimate Amazon only has the cheapest copy about 75% of the time (again, an estimation).

Even compared to just a year ago, the potential for finding cheaper copies of books on sites other than Amazon has doubled (third disclaimer: *just my estimation*).

Profit method #3: Amazon-to-book-buy-back-sites.

Now you're starting to see how this works, and I won't need to go into as much detail from this point.

Believe it or not, Amazon-to-buy-back-site trades are the most common of all. And you get cash (not credit). So these aren't just better, they're more abundant.

There is huge fluctuation among buy back site prices, and the cash buy back value is very often well beyond Amazon's trade-in value.

The trick here is simple: Run books from Amazon's trade-in store through book buy back offer comparison sites. There are two: BookScouter.com and BookFinder.com/buyback.

You might be wondering: Why are we looking for books in Amazon's trade-in store to run through buy back sites, if we're not trading in to Amazon? Why not look for books on the entirety of Amazon?

Simple answer: It is very rare to see a buy back site offer for any book that is not also in the Amazon trade-in store. Of all trade-in style platforms, Amazon's is by far the biggest. You'll see book buy back sites with as many as 100,000 offers, yet Amazon's book trade-in offers alone can be over 300,000.

So if it's in Amazon's trade-in store, there's a good chance at least one buy back site is offering money for it. If you're just cruising the rest of Amazon randomly, the rate is probably 1 in 200.

This game is all about increasing efficiency, so I strongly recommend you do all your searching inside the Amazon trade-in store.

Profit method #4: Bookfinder-to-buy-back-site

Same formula as #3, only this time we're sourcing books from any site *except* Amazon, using BookFinder.com. This lets us find the cheapest copy virtually anywhere on the internet, and get the highest cash profits for our books.

Searching Other Sites With 1-Click Using "Context Search"

Before we get to the step-by-step system, I'm going to outline how to install and configure a simple tool that will let you run price comparisons, scan for book buy back values, and probably a lot more I haven't even figured out yet, all with one click.

The solution is a simple browser extension called "Context Search." This innocuously-named tool allows to you run any highlighted text through any website you tell it to as a search, with one click.

As an example let's say you wanted to run an ISBN through BookScouter.com to scan over 30 cash buy back sites for the highest offer. Here is what you would have to do *without* Context Search:

1. Copy the ISBN
2. Open a new tab
3. Go to BookScouter.com
4. Paste the ISBN
5. Hit search

If you're trying to search dozens of hundreds of books in a sitting, this is time prohibitive. It will simply slow you down way too much.

Here's how it works with Context Search:

1. Highlight & right-click the ISBN
2. Click the BookScouter link in Context Search

That's it.

It's the next best thing to just having Amazon embed all the useful links we need right on the trade-in store page.

How to install Context Search

There are a few steps to getting it installed. They're a little weird, but if you follow each step exactly as I outline, this will be done in a couple minutes.

1. **Install Context Search:** The extension is available free in both the Chrome and Firefox extension stores.

2. **Create a folder in your bookmarks:** Go to your browser bookmarks menu. Create a folder and name it "Searches." Yes I know this is weird, but do exactly that (to the letter).

3. **Do a search for an item (any item) in every site you want to readily access:** I'm going to give you my short list here. You may want to add to it.

1. BooksFinder.com
2. BookFinder.com/buyback

This is the most basic list. You'll want to add to this based on your interest in searching in other categories, or even knowing of sites I haven't discovered myself yet.

Whatever sites you add, they will fall into one of these two categories:

1. Price comparisons sites (finding the cheapest copy).
2. Trade-in or buy back sites (to get the most for your item).

To restate, you're taking an ISBN and doing a search for that ISBN in both of those sites. It doesn't matter which ISBN, but this step is very important.

This is where it gets a little weirder, but follow the steps exactly and this will be very simple.

4. **Alter the URL**

After you do a search for any product at the sites of your choosing, look at the URL. I mean, literally look at it in the URL field at the top of the browser. Find the ISBN (or UPC or other identifier if you're outside of books) in the URL. Delete it from the URL field. And replace *just the ISBN* with this:

"%s" (no quotes)

Literally replace the ISBN with "%s." Don't ask me why. This is just how its done.

5. **Bookmark this new, altered URL**

Now you need to bookmark that *exact* URL with that small change you just made.

But there's one small problem: Your browser (at least *my* browser) won't let you bookmark a site unless you're actually on that site and its fully loaded. In other words, you can't just change the text and bookmark it. You have to hit return to go to that URL first.

Except that URL doesn't exist. If you just hit return to go to that URL, BookFinder will alter it to something else. It will undo our change.

But I found a way around that: Turn off your wifi or internet. Disable it. Smash the router. Whatever you have to do. Just turn off the internet.

Now hit return with that URL you just altered in the browser URL field. It will show "page not found" or something, because your internet is off. But now you can bookmark it. You've tricked your browser.

Do that for both URLs.

Now take both URLs and drag them to your new bookmarks folder called "Search."

Now you're set. What you just did is added these special links to Context Search, so any text you highlight you can run through these sites with one click.

To confirm you did this correctly, highlight any text, and when you right click it and select the Context Search option, both URLs should show. Just like the image below. Now you can run the highlighted text as a search with one click.

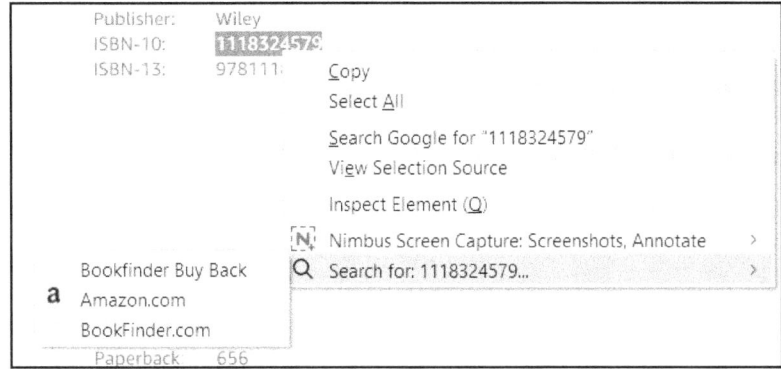

This will save a ton of time, will make your searches a lot more elegant, and is basically mandatory for the system I'm about to give you…

A Step-By-Step Trade-In & Buy Back Site Arbitrage Search

This is the chapter where it all comes together. Let's do a live search for profit in Amazon's trade-in store.

By "live," I mean I'm actually going through the steps I'm explaining here in real time, and posting screenshots of the results. (And if somehow you don't believe I really did this search, I'll be emailing you raw footage of it a couple days after you download this book).

Step One: Go To The Amazon Trade-In Store

Google "Amazon Trade-In."

Next step: Choose A Category

Amazon's trade-in store has several hundred thousand items. Choose a category.

This is actually not that simple. As of the time of this writing, Amazon has changed their trade-in store layout and removed a link for "Books." The closest we can get is "Textbooks," which brings up about 1/3 of total books. However once you're in the Textbooks category, look in the left hand column. You'll see the option to select the entire Books category.

It is by far easier for this formula to work in Books than other categories, simply because its easier to comb the internet for cheaper copies of books than other products (as we'll discuss). But the basics of this formula will work in all categories.

From this point, we'll assume you're searching Books.

(Optional) Next step: Select A Search Keyword

By default, Amazon is going to display the most high-demand books on the first page. This isn't a bad thing, but we can do better. We're trying to avoid going over the same books other people are going over .(Realistically, this book is going to be read by thousands of people. But most people are lazy, and won't apply this keyword search suggestion. That means everyone will crowd the first couple pages with these tricks, and you'll want to get outside of the results everyone else is combing through.)

Literally any word will do. You're just trying to get outside the first few pages.

Since we're going for the most high value books (we'll get to this in a second), it would be strategic to choose keywords that point to textbooks (generally the most expensive books). It's pretty easy to Google "academic fields of study" to get a list of niche keywords that will point to textbooks.

Don't overthink this part. Any keyword will do.

Next step: Look For Books For Sale Cheaper Than Their Trade-in Value

There's no magic wand here: You just start searching.

Are we really just randomly combing through the trade-in store? Is there any way to make this more efficient?

Yes. Experience has taught the odds of a book having an offer below the trade-in value goes up at pace with the trade-in value - higher the trade-in value, higher the chance you'll find a profitable copy. This isn't a complex economic quirk, its actually pretty simple logic: Higher the value, the more wiggle room there is for price fluctuations. And a certain percentage of those price fluctuations will be to your advantage.

My advice: Look for books with trade-in value of $50 and up. Don't adhere to this figure as gospel, its just a solid rule of thumb.

Now let's start clicking on books and checking prices...

Option #1 is the click on the title of every book in the trade-in store. This will bring up the product page, where you can see the price of the book. Downside of this is that it opens in the same tab, so as you click around it can become easy to lose your place, and you'll always have to hit the back button to get back to the trade-in store.

Option #2 is to right click the title, and select "open link in new tab."

In this live example, the very first book that displayed (without even choosing a keyword) was called: *Materials Science & Engineering.*

Clicking over to view the book's product page brings us here:

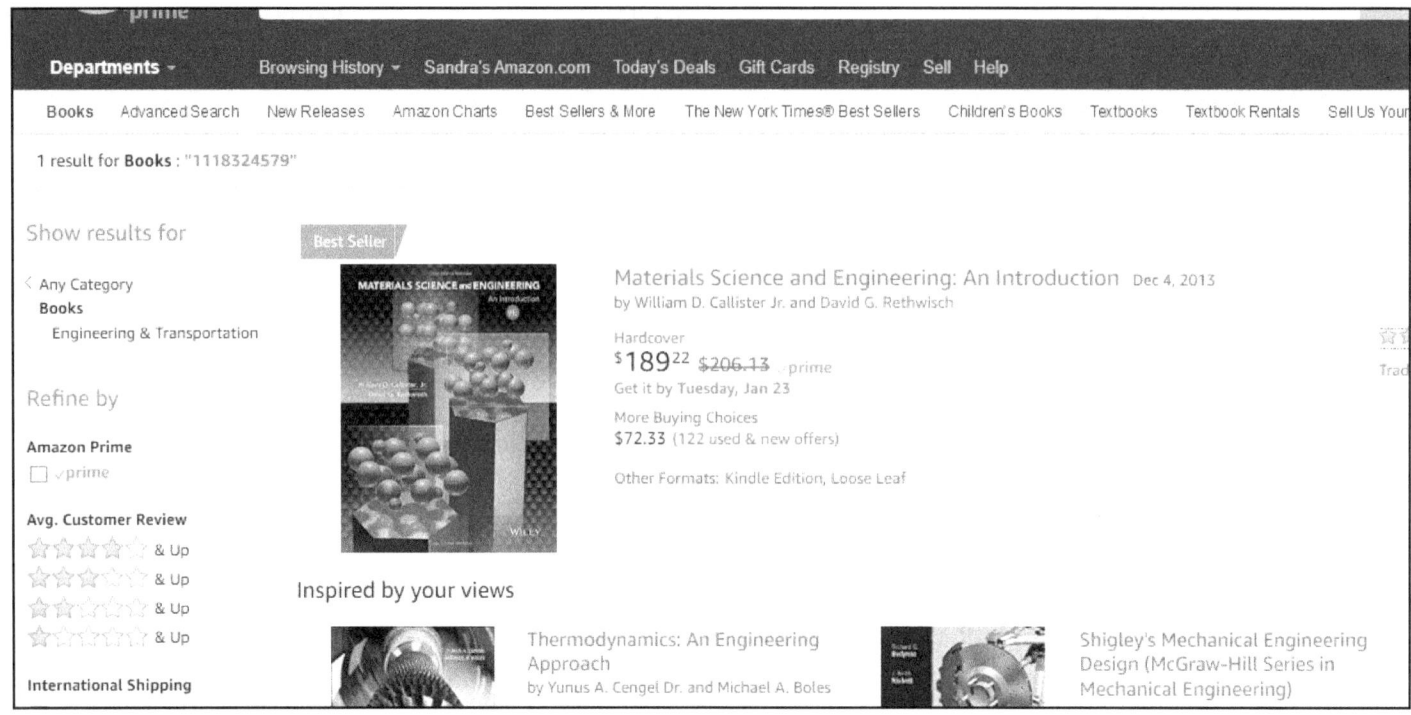

This is looking good. Do you see what I see? Look towards the middle of that image.

The lowest selling price is *below* the trade-in value. The trade-in value is $127.95, and the lowest price to purchase is $72.33. This is exactly the kind of offer we're looking for.

Next step: Scrutinize The Offers

Looks good, but we're not in the clear yet. We have to verify the offer(s) for sale below the trade-in value is one that can be submitted to Amazon and won't be rejected. Refer to the "What Can Go Wrong?" chapter for the full list, but the most common reasons books are rejected are certain damage Amazon won't allow, and the dreaded "International Editions." So we have to scrutinize the offer(s).

Here is what we see:

Trade-In Arbitrage

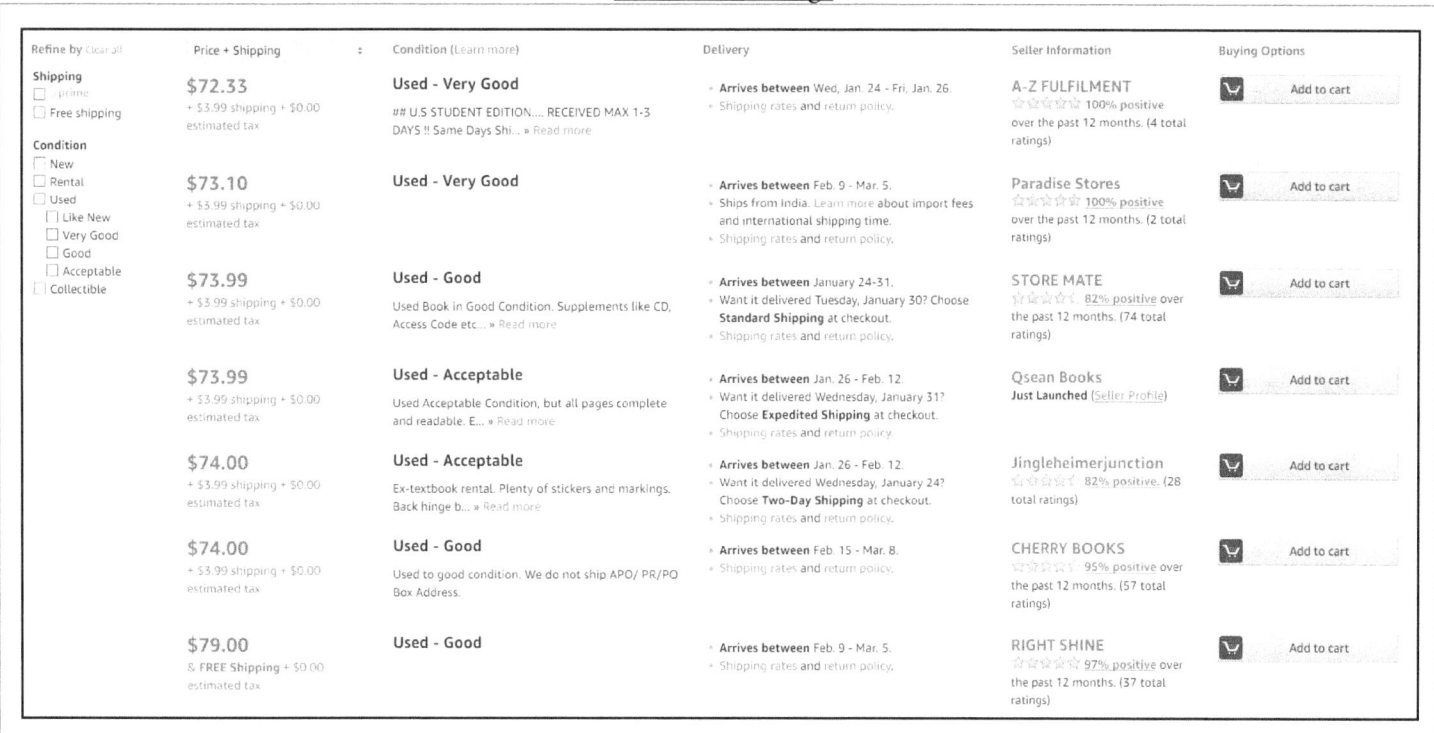

This is looking even better.

Generally when you find a book cheaper than the trade-in value, it is one lone offer that was listed by a rogue (or more likely: sloppy) seller.

With this book, we can see *seven* listings that are priced below the trade-in value (actually more outside this image). How does this happen? Is everyone insane? What is going on? As we covered, the trade-in value is inherently less than the true "market value" of the book. So how can seven sellers be so lazy (or reckless or clueless) as to price their copies this low?

More than likely, there's a simple answer: One (insert: lazy/reckless/clueless) seller priced their offer low, and the other six had automatic repricing software simply follow them blindly. In all its hilarity, that's how most Amazon repricing works. It's run by robots.

We have to look closer and make sure the book we want to purchase will be accepted by Amazon. Contrary to what you might think, Amazon will take some seriously beat up books for trade-in, but they won't take everything. See the "What Can Go Wrong" chapter on all the details, but suffice to say there are a few hurdles we need to clear before we can call this a success.

Primarily we're looking for 1. any damage to the book that is on Amazon's short list of things they won't accept, and 2. the dreaded "international editions." There are other things, but those are the top two.

You can never be 100% sure a seller won't make an inaccurate listing, but everything with this book checks out: The cheapest listing is in Very Good condition, with no indication its an international edition. Everything looks good.

Next Step: Lock In The Trade-in Price

Most people at this point will skip to the next step ("Check Cash Buy Back Sites"). You have to promise me you won't be one of them unless you want to avoid credit entirely and only deal in cash (I don't blame you). Here's why: Amazon trade-in prices are extremely volatile, fluctuating wildly all the time. A book can have a trade-in value of $147 one minute, that will plummet to $60 in literally 10 seconds. You think I'm embellishing, but if you do this for any length of time you'll have an offer vanish before your eyes because you delayed a few seconds, and you'll wish you'd listened.

As *soon* as you verify there is at least one copy for sale that will allow you to profit (if not before), lock it in. Hit the "trade-in" button, go through the steps, and freeze that price. Remember you are not entering into a legal contract. There is no penalty for not sending in the book if something goes wrong. You can just cancel the submission later.

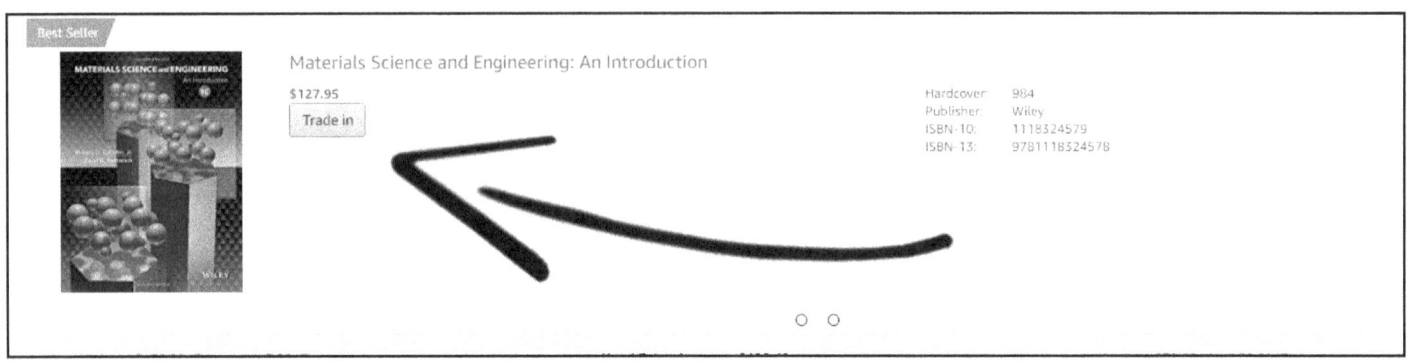

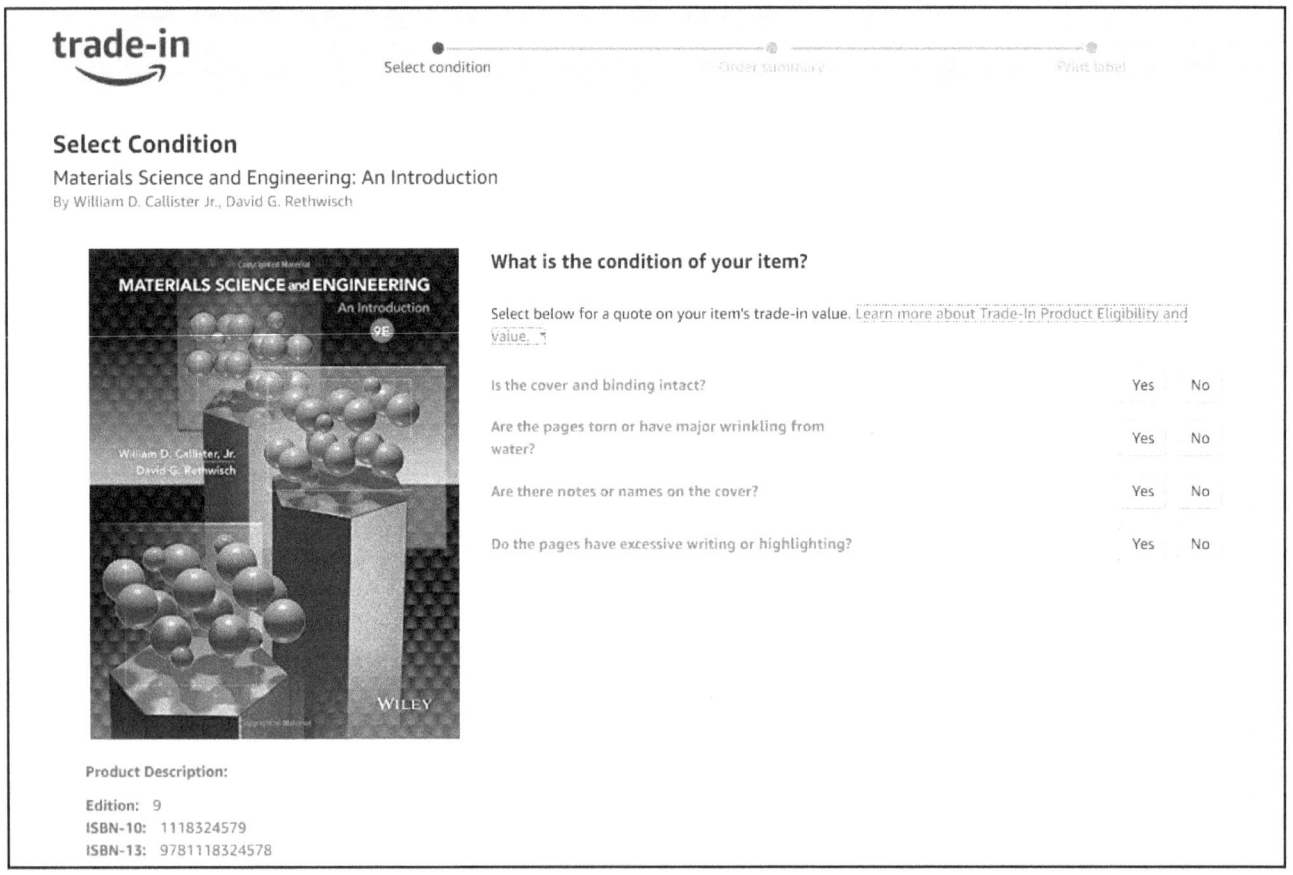

Next Step: Find The Highest Cash Buy Back Value

There's always a (quite good) chance we can get more in cash than Amazon credit. Now we scan over 30 cash buy back sites with one click. This is where we make first use of the Context Search extension I covered in a previous chapter. Assuming you got that set up properly, you will be able to highlight and right-click any text, and the BookFinder.com or BookScouter.com link will show in the context search menu (either is fine).

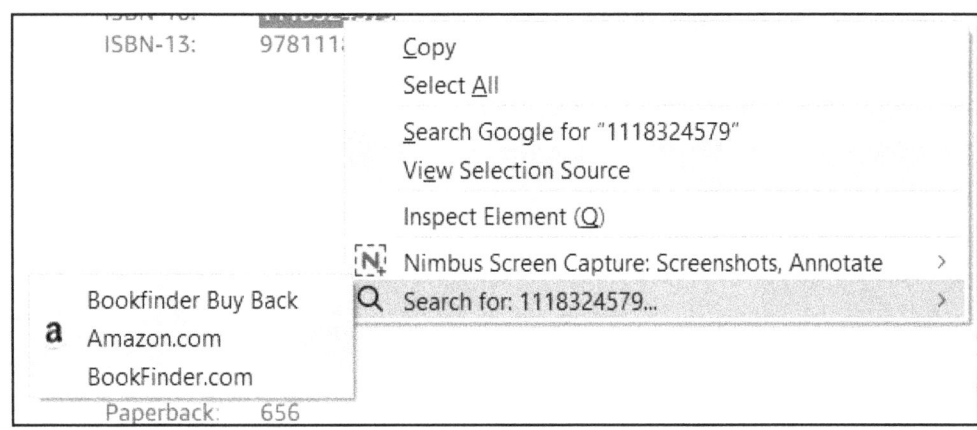

Here's what we see:

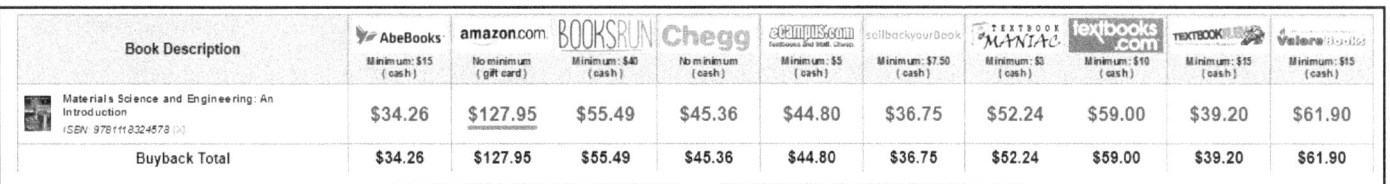

To translate, Amazon is the highest offer for this book, cash or credit. Even if we wanted cash, there aren't any buy back offers for more than the selling price on Amazon, so Amazon credit it is.

There's still hope for us doing a straight cash transaction using this next step…

Next step: Find The Cheapest Copy Online

We're using the Context Search extension for this step as well, also with BookFinder.com. Only difference is, we're scanning BookFinder.com, not BookFinder.com/buyback.

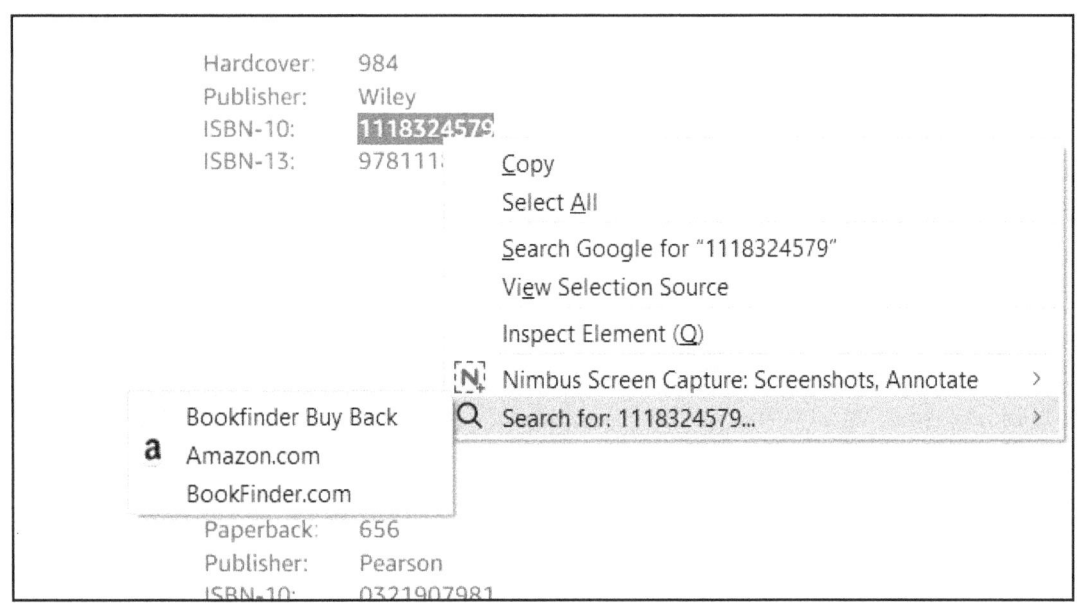

Click the Bookfinder link and it will open a new tab showing all offers for that book across 40 bookselling sites. The one at the top is the cheapest copy just about anywhere online (including eBay).

Rough numbers here, but in my experience Amazon is the cheapest copy online about 75% of the time, and Bookfinder will save you money about 25%. So savings from this extra step can really add up, and make otherwise unprofitable books actually profitable.

This search shows reveals that Amazon is the cheapest for this book.

Note: The perils of "international editions" are much greater when sourcing from outside of Amazon, so be extra vigilant.

Next Step: Buy The Book

I'm sure you can figure this part out.

Amazon let's you submit two copies per trade-in offer (sometimes more, it's weird). If you have the money, and there's more than one copy available, buy two copies.

At this stage, it would be great if we could have the seller ship it directly to Amazon or the buy back site, but that's not how it works. You'll have the book shipped either to you, or a prep service (see "Using Prep Services To Partially Automating Your Trade-In Business.")

Important detail if you're shipping to Amazon: You must print off the shipping label from your trade-in account in 7 days, or Amazon will remove it from your account. You can ship within 21 days, but you have to print that shipping label ASAP.

So print the shipping label as soon as you buy the book. Ship it whenever you receive it.

(Rules with buy back sites vary wildly, so if you're submitting to one, take note of how long you have to ship.)

Next Step: Receive The Book & See If The Trade-in or Buy Back Value Has Gone Up

This is an important step that will make you money about half the time.

Trade-in and buy back values fluctuate like crazy all the time. They go up, they go down, they go sideways - often many times in the same day. The one thing they don't do is stay the same.

This means that by the time your book arrives, there's a 50/50 chance the value will have gone down. This is irrelevant, because you've already locked in the value.

This also means there's a 50/50 chance the value has gone *up*. This is great news, because this new higher amount is the amount we're going to get. But Amazon or the buy back site isn't just going to give it to us. We have to ask for it.

If you check and find the trade-in or cash value of your book has gone up, here's what you do:

1. Cancel the current submission.
2. Resubmit at the higher price.

More free money.

Next Step: Ship It In

Amazon (and most buy back sites) give you a pre-paid shipping label, so you'll just affix it to the envelope and take it to any UPS drop off location.

With Amazon, they will tell you you have 7 days to ship the book, but the reality is you have 21 days. 7 days is the "official" deadline, but they will honor the trade-in amount for 7 days.

This detail is huge for us, because a good percentage of books will not arrive in 7 days.

Next Step: Get Paid

Give a week or so for the book to arrive and be processed, and you'll get an email letting you know the trade-in credit or cash has been deposited in your Amazon or PayPal account (some do things a little differently, but this applies to most).

Some sellers, for some books, will be given Amazon credit instantly, even before the book is shipped.

Next Step: Decide Your Next Move

- Roll the credit into more credit?
- Roll the credit into books the sell for cash on Amazon?
- Blow the credit on dog toys?

Up to you. But the hardest part (which wasn't very hard) is behind you: You just took a small amount of money and turned it into a larger amount of money. Just like magic.

The Top 8 Trade-In Arbitrage Tricks

Let's get even deeper. Here are eight tricks to keep in mind as you search.

#1: Speed-searching: Increase efficiency 10x by analyzing prices to know when you should click over to BookFinder.com

We talked about how the best opportunity is in using BookFinder.com to scan over 40 bookselling sites. But should you click over every for every single book? How do you know what books to click on and which will almost certainly have no opportunity?

There's a couple of tricks.

First, I have to reiterate there is potential for *any* book to have room for profit. Literally any book. But if you want to increase efficiency, here's is what you do:

One, only click over on the highest priced books.

Two, focus on any book for which the sales price is close to the trade-in price. Prices on other sites tend to stay within range of the prices on Amazon. That doesn't mean they match to the penny, it means they stay "close." (Again, generally). Part of this is just general "efficient market" phenomenon, part of it is repricing software that sets prices on 3rd party sites to match Amazon's. It's just how things work.

So let's hypothetically say you're skimming through the Amazon trade-in store and see 19 books with $100 trade-in value each selling for $200. Then let's say the 20th has $100 trade-in value but it is selling for $130. There is a much better chance of finding that $130 book cheaper than $100 on a 3rd party site than those other 19 books combined.

When the sales price is close (I measure "close" by within 1/3) to the trade-in value, there's a dramatically higher likelihood of profit.

#2: Don't ignore razor thin margins, because the profit is guaranteed

Let's assume you're currently in the business of selling books (versus trading them in). You probably have rigid ROI standards (expecting to double your investment, triple, etc).

Do not apply those standards to trade-in arbitrage. This is a different game, with different rules.

Remember the reasons you have those ROI standards to begin with: To buffer against prices dropping, to buffer against Amazon commission, to buffer against long term storage fees, and more.

None of those apply with Amazon's trade-in program: The price is set in stone, there are no commissions, and there are no fees.

Would you pay $50 for a book you would only make $5 on if you sold it on Amazon? No chance. The margins are too thin.

But with trade-in, most potential for uncertainty is accounted for, and that $5 is virtually guaranteed.

It's an entirely different way of thinking. Whereas your usual buying test goes:

"Will this allow me room for profit when all the smoke clears and buffer me against the potential for a loss?"

…it shifts entirely to this test:

"Is this fixed, guaranteed amount worth my time?"

As an example, the total time cost for that $5 profit book is the time it takes you to checkout, then put it in an envelope and affix the Amazon shipping label. Assuming you're already going to the UPS store to drop off other books, the actual time cost is only a few minutes.

Those $3 and $5 profit books can really add up.

#3: Profit off timing your trades & hacking price fluctuations

Timing your trades is a big part of this game. There are two sides to this: Knowing when prices to buy books are lowest, and knowing when trade-in values are highest.

This is a more advanced tactic, employing "timed trades" by analyzing two things:

1. When sales prices are lowest.
2. When trade-in values are highest.

When we know these things, we buy at the cheapest possible price, and hold off on submitting the book until we know the trade-in value will be highest. We do this by relying on historical trade-in data to time our trades.

Some bad news: There's only one tool that does this, and its not free. Because I've committed to keeping all the tactics in this book relevant without the use of paid tools, I won't be spending time on timed trades here. But I do have an upcoming chapter on this where I give you the broad stokes.

#4: The best opportunity is in the more expensive books

The biggest opportunities are with books in the $50+ range. It's infinitely easier to find a book with $125 trade-in value you can find on another site for $110 than a book with $30 trade-in value you can find elsewhere for $15.

#5: Know how to turn Amazon trade-in credit into cash

If you can master online book arbitrage, and know how to turn $100 in trade credit into $1,000 (or more), you basically rule the world.

I'm dedicating a whole chapter to this.

#6: Use Price Proximity to Find Underpriced Books To Sell For Cash

And I'm dedicating a whole chapter to this too, but the basic idea is: You can search Amazon's trade in store, and instead of looking for offers lower than their trade-in value, you look for offers with prices *close* to their trade-in value. This often indicates an item is priced artificially low, and can be purchased and quickly resold on Amazon for cash.

#7 Use Book Buy Back Sites

Too many people think trade-in arbitrage is all about Amazon trade-in. Cash buy back sites are even better.

#8: Buy Two Copies.

Amazon will take two copies of all books (as far as I've seen). That means if you think you found an opportunity that pays you $25, it's really paying you $50. Not all buy back sites will take more than one copy, but Amazon always will.

Timed Trades: Profiting Off Amazon Price Fluctuations

The premise is a simple one, in two parts:

Premise #1: Trade-in values are fluctuating all the time. Amazon is one giant algorithm, and that algorithm is constantly adjusting trade-in values based on numerous factors.

If you can hold your books and trade them in when you know historically trade-in value are highest, you can get the highest return.

Premise #2: Prices of third party offers on Amazon are fluctuating just the same. Going up, going down. Not because of Amazon algorithm, because of normal buying and selling activity.

If you buy your books when you know historically they are lowest, you can pay the least.

It's gets better…

What if you could both buy books when they're cheapest, and "sell" when trade-in value is highest? What if you could increase the gap between the buying price and the trade-in price to the widest possible spread, by knowing the historical data?

There is a little-known pattern to trade-in values – both when they tend to go up, and when they tend to go down. If you know what these dates are, you can time both your purchases and trades to buy low and then trade-in when the prices peak.

Yes, this can be done.

How awesome would be it be if we knew the exact date books were cheapest, and the exact date trade-in values are highest? Then we could do all our buying on one day, all our trading on another day, and make a killing?

It's *almost* that simple, but not quite. Because pricing trends affect various books differently, we can't just memorize a couple dates and exploit this trick to the fullest.

While textbooks tend to have peaks of trade-in value and valleys (no pun intended) of price in the same windows of time, there are many textbooks that don't follow these rules. Certain textbooks have different peak sales and low sales windows, and naturally that affects their trade-in value and price.

One example to illustrate the complexity: Test study guides for the "Multi-state Bar Exam" (MBE). At a glance these appear to be regular textbooks, but they peak (and valley) at totally different times than other textbooks. This exam only happens at the end of July and January, which affects their pricing fluctuations. Trade-in values tend to peak a little before the test, and prices tend to plummet after.

Every book has its own pricing history. So there's way more than can be shared in one article (or one book).

The best you can hope to memorize is the broad strokes. Which I'm about to reveal…

How did I get acquainted with Amazon pricing and trade-in history?

I mentioned this in a previous chapter, but over at Zen Arbitrage (book arbitrage tool for selling books, not as powerful for trade-in) we have a massive data harvesting system churning through tens of millions of products on Amazon daily. Among it all is trade-in data for virtually every book in Amazon's trade-in store, going back over two years.

So I dug around and pulled up some numbers, and am presenting them to you here.

Historical pricing history gold #1: When Amazon trade-in value are highest.

Highest trade-in values for textbooks: First 12 days of August.

Analysis: The numbers here are sightly weird in that there is no single "big date" within the first two weeks that is far and away the one where trade-in values spike to a crazy degree. Values are, generally speaking, a lot higher across the beginning of the month.

Second place: December 26th.

Analysis: For textbooks, trade-in prices the day after Christmas surge to levels 70% above normal (on average). As far as single days of the year, December 26th is THE day to submit books to Amazon's trade-in program.

Both of these windows / dates makes sense, because textbook sales peak shortly after each of these ranges, and Amazon wants to stock up just before (not during) the sales rush.

Sidenote: As a quick example of how wildly this varies depending on the type of book, I noticed with "Gift"-type books (box sets, etc) trade-in values are highest the first week of December

Historical pricing history gold #2: When Amazon textbook prices are lowest

Trade-in credit mining and arbitrage is not just for textbooks. But the Amazon trade-in store leans heavily towards textbooks, so historical textbook pricing data is of chief relevance to trade-in.

In our database, we store pricing data a little differently than trade-in, so I pulled up the top 30 dates where textbook prices were lowest.

Lowest textbook prices: 11 of the 30 lowest days of the year were in December.

Before pulling these numbers, I suspected December had the lowest prices (sales of textbooks are also lowest in early-to-mid December) but I didn't know it was so severe that 1/3 of the examples of a book's lowest price were in a single month.

Now, there's lots of different ways to slice and dice the numbers. I just looked at the 30 lowest dates and noticed the highest concentration was in December. There are certainly more statistically sound ways to do this, but I'm not a statistician.

What does all this mean?

Two actionable (and profitable) takeaways here:

1. If you're buying textbooks, the time to buy is:

- Mid-December

If you have a textbook, the times to trade it in are (usually):

- Early-August.
- December 26th. (More generally, late-December).

Of course there's opportunity all year around, but if you had to pick a 2-week window where the best action is, it would be roughly December 12th to the 26th. December is the best time to hunt for Amazon trade-in opportunity: Prices on textbooks are at their lowest 11 days of the month (based on the single year I looked at), and trade-in values are highest December 26th (same disclaimer).

So there you go. You can make a lot of money with that one.

S/he with the best data wins.

The Only Two Ways To Really Mess Up Trade-In Arbitrage

So I've mentioned many times this is a *mostly* risk free way to profit on Amazon. If I said "mostly," what is the limited risk? Here are only two major ways to screw up trade-in credit arbitrage:

1. Buying books that get rejected by Amazon or the buy back site (primarily heavily damaged books, or "international editions.")
2. Shipping a book in past the deadline.

Buying the dreaded "international edition"

When you're buying books outside of Amazon (this happens less on Amazon), there's a ton of unscrupulous sellers selling the cursed "international editions." Without going into the details of what these are, they can't be sold on Amazon, and can't be traded into Amazon. Shady sellers will use creative language to shroud the fact their books are international editions, using terms like "global edition" (among others). Any time you find a book for sale that is cheaper than the trade-in value, you have to scrutinize the listing closely to insure it is not an international edition.

Buying the wrong edition

Related to this, similarly unscrupulous sellers will list older editions or custom editions under the ISBN for the current edition. This can be determined in a couple ways: One, the cover will look different (older edition) or will mention the name of a specific school. Two, if there's no photo, check the description to be sure the edition number matches with the one Amazon is offering trade-in credit for, and that there is no mention of it being a "custom edition."

Both of these can usually be assessed at a 1.5 second glance.

Buying a damaged book

Next is shipping a damaged book. Every book buyback site has its own list of what it will and won't accept. Amazon itself is actually pretty liberal, and allows a certain amount of damage and highlighting.

However, Amazon will not accept a book for which any of the following applies:

- Library copy
- Custom edition textbooks (typically has a school name listed)
- Water damaged (wavy, swollen or discolored, crinkled, stains, rings)
- Heavy highlighting
- Broken spine or binding
- Books with torn or taped cover
- Missing, torn, or loose pages
- Burns, fire, or smoke damage
- Strong odor of any kind (including musty odor, cigar or cigarette odor)

- Marked "Not for Resale" (or is otherwise marked not for sale) anywhere on the cover or inside

You can't protect against every seller who may not grade their books accurately. But this risk can be significantly mitigated by scrutinizing conditions descriptions closely and avoiding any that look ambiguous or outright sketchy.

Here's a trick that will greatly reduce the rate at which you receive damaged books or international editions. Every time you order a book, send this email to the seller:

"I have just purchased (textbook) from you and I only want the U.S. Student edition in the condition that you stated in the item description including matching the ASIN exactly. I will not accept any International, Instructor, or alternate versions of this book. I will also not accept a book that has significant damage or blemishes not described."

This can puts the seller on notice: *I'm watching you. Don't pull any shenanigans.*

Shipping a book past the deadline

Amazon gives you 21 days to ship your book before they void the submission (remember, they tell you you have 7 days, you really have 21). Book buy back sites vary (remember, there's over 30 of them).

Almost all books will arrive to you before the 21 days. If you're dealing with a tighter book buy back site schedule, you can reduce the risk of missing a deadline by paying attention to the offer you're buying. Is it shipping from overseas? A lot offers do. Avoid those.

You can't control when a seller ships your book. And you can't control when a book arrives. The only thing you can control is how long after you receive the book that you ship it. So if you're approaching the deadline, get it out fast.

Profiting Off Categories Other Than Books

Amazon has a lot more than books in its trade-in store.

Here's a list of the categories:

- CDs & Vinyl
- Movies & TV
- Electronics
- Cell Phones & Accessories
- Video Games
- Toys & Games
- Sports & Outdoors
- Office Products
- Software
- Automotive Parts & Accessories
- Arts, Crafts & Sewing
- Health, Household & Baby Care
- Home & Kitchen
- Beauty & Personal Care
- Tools & Home Improvement
- Home & Business Services
- Industrial & Scientific
- Musical Instruments
- Clothing, Shoes & Jewelry
- Garden & Outdoor
- Baby
- Pet Supplies
- Everything Else
- Kindle Accessories
- Grocery & Gourmet Food
- Appliances

This list is very misleading, because most of these categories (like Grocery) have only a small handful of offers that are probably only there by accident. The vast majority of all trade-in offers are in Books, CDs, Movies, Electronics & Video Games.

These numbers will fluctuate a lot, but as of the time of this writing, these are the numbers of offers in each category:

- CDs & vinyl: 100,000+
- DVDs: 100,000+
- Electronics: 30,000+

- Cell phones & accessories: 10,000+
- Video games: 10,000+
- Software: 500+

The vast majority of everything else in every other category are products that are mis-categorized, and belong in one of the above categories. For example, most trade-in offers in Toys are actually video games.

So is there money to made in other categories? Yes and no. It won't go quite as easily as with books. The primary differences are:

Absence of cash buy back sites
Books have the huge benefit of having over 30 cash buy back sites. A few categories (like video games) have cash buy back sites, most don't. Meaning Amazon trade-in is your only option.

Absence of price comparison sites
Most categories do have some way to compare across many sites, but they require you to search by UPC, which isn't always easy to get from Amazon. This adds a couple steps to the process, because you have to get the UPC (more on that in a moment).

Trade-in values that are too low to profit
The vast majority of all offers in all categories in Amazon's trade-in store are for under $10. In other words, there is not room for profit and they aren't even worth scrutinizing. The highest values outside of Books are in Electronics and Video Games.

Cash buy back sites for non-books

Here are sites where you can sell non-book items for cash:

- Electronics: Gazelle, Best Buy, or Nextworth.
- DVDs: Decluttr, SecondSpin
- CDs: Decluttr
- Video Games: Decluttr , SecondSpin, CashForGamers.

Price comparison sites

These are the BookFinder's of non-book categories. The first two links are easy to add to Context Search. PriceGrabber doesn't work as well.

- CDs: GetCDPrices.com
- DVDs: GetDVDPrices.com
- Video Games: PriceCharting.com
- Everything Else: PriceGrabber.com

How to get the UPC code

If you want to do some hardcore price comparison buy back offer comparison shopping outside of Amazon, you'll run into the issue of how to efficiently search. On just about any site, the options you'll be given are to search by product name, or by UPC.

Searching by name is problematic because different sites use different product names for the same product, and just copying the product title from Amazon will inevitably either bring up no results, or filter out results you do what. There's just too much variation, and too many redudant and only slighlty different product pages for virtually the same item. Don't even bother searching by name.

The only option that will directly match you with the product you're looking at on Amazon is the UPC. Problem is, most of the time Amazon won't show the UPC (depends on the product category). The only unique identifier you have is the ASIN (Amazon's version of a UPC). How do you find out the UPC if all you have is an ASIN?

The answer is a free online ASIN-to-UPC converter. Copy the ASIN, paste it in, and it gives you the UPC. There are a few, but the simplest one I've found is:

www.asinlab.com/asin-to-upc

The cool weird thing about DVDs

One thing stuck out to me when I was reviewing the numbers on trade-in data:

Prices of DVDs on Amazon drop below their trade-in value at a rate of 4-to-1 compared to Books.

Meaning the step-by-step formula outlined in this book actually works a lot better with DVDs.

The downsides are that the average trade-in value is much lower than books, and there's less of them. So your average take will be less than $10, but its a lot easier to find those opportunities as well.

Only difference in the formula is that you have to add GetDVDprices.com to your Context Search list, letting you find the cheapest copy of the DVD online.

Price Proximity And The Underpriced Book Hack

Introducing "Price Proximity": How to exploit Amazon trade-in credit arbitrage to identify underpriced books you can sell for quick cash (and skip trade-in credit altogether)

From my first mention of "trade-in arbitrage" on FBAmastery.com, the biggest question I got was:

Why would you trade a book in for credit when you can sell it for even more cash?

I've addressed this point several times in this book, but I'll repeat to make this totally clear:

Amazon trade-in credit arbitrage appeals to a certain kind of risk-averse seller who wants quick results and minimal risk.

That may not be you (it's usually not me), but I wrote this book because I realize there's a ton of Amazon sellers who simply can't stand the uncertainty of Amazon price volatility and often long turnaround times. They want quick results. (If you've made it this far in the book, I'm assuming this applies to you). What's more, there are tons of people who don't want to bother with being Amazon sellers at all: They want something fast without the infrastructure of an Amazon seller's account.

The trade-off here is that *trade-in value is always less than the true market value of the book*. Otherwise, the amount Amazon is offering for a book would be lower.

Yet there are also sellers who want to have their cake and eat it too: Minimal risk *and* the full market value for their books.

This chapter is about how Amazon trade-in can work for both types. Do you roll your eyes at the prospect of hunting for Amazon trade-in because you're selling yourself short? This trick is for you.

Price Proximity: How to use trade-in credit to get quick cash (and skip trade-in altogether)

Let's get into a simple formula for using trade-in credit tactics to identify severely underpriced books, and sell them for quick cash (either FBA or merchant fulfilled). This involves what I call "Price Proximity."

Here's the general formula (we'll get more specific in a moment):

1. Hunt for trade-in credit opportunity just like you would if you wanted trade-in credit.
2. But instead, use the trade-in amount as baseline value which indicates you sell the book at a significantly higher number than the trade-in amount.
3. Sell the book and get paid in cash.

So here's how "Price Proximity" works:

Anytime you find a book in the trade-in store that you can buy on Amazon or 3rd party site for *close* to the trade-in value (say, within 20% or 30%), that's a very strong indication one of two things is happening:

1. The trade-in value is unusually high.
2. The sales price is unusually low.

If it's #2, this means it can be sold at a much higher value for quick cash. In other words, a selling price that is within close proximity to Amazon's trade-in price is strong indicator that book significantly underpriced. I.e. artificially low.

So as someone who wants to sell books for cash, what you're doing here is using the tactics of the Amazon trade-in hunter to find these underpriced books, and convert them into extremely low-risk cash transactions.

Fact: The Amazon trade-in value is generally more than 30% below the average selling price

I did a quick search in Zen Arbitrage for books with trade-in value. Here's a screenshot to illustrate the point (trade-in value is the far right column, used prices on the left):

	Used	New	Amazon	FBA	Trade
Abnormal Psychology	$155.17	$232.84	no offer	🔍	$109.90
Criminal Procedure, Investigating Crime (...	$138.00	$185.40	$185.40	🔍	$109.68
Design of Reinforced Concrete	$184.90	$189.00	$194.99	🔍	$109.40
Fundamentals of Advanced Accounting	$157.97	$174.15	$179.45	🔍	$109.30
First Amendment Law (University Casebo...	$149.99	$171.29	$171.29	🔍	$109.26
Auditing and Assurance Services Plus My...	$250.92	$292.10	$296.10	🔍	$109.20
Geosystems: An Introduction to Physical ...	$127.88	$170.94	$170.94	🔍	$108.90
Business Analysis and Valuation: Using Fi...	$149.42	$199.88	$201.28	🔍	$108.70
Corporate Finance: The Core (4th Edition)...	$164.65	$219.99	$248.13	🔍	$108.40
Atlas of Regional and Free Flaps for Head...	$228.90	$246.23	$246.23	🔍	$108.32
DeGarmo's Materials and Processes in M...	$155.50	$155.50	$159.56	🔍	$108.20
The Principal: Creative Leadership for Ex...	$181.88	$183.59	$188.45	🔍	$107.98
Financial Institutions Management: A Risk...	$142.00	$148.74	$152.74	🔍	$107.96
Anatomy & Physiology (6th Edition)	$148.99	$207.65	$209.82	🔍	$107.80
Introduction to Nuclear Engineering (4th E...	$184.99	$223.20	$238.21	🔍	$107.80

How do we know historically what a book's "real" value is? A: Keepa

Of course, no one can predict the ultimate selling price of any book. But we can look at historical data to make a calculated estimation about the lowest amount that book is ever likely to sell for, and hedge our bets using that as a baseline.

The answer to the question of a book's "real" value is the Keepa browser extension. Keepa shows historical pricing data, including six and twelve month averages.

(Go install Keepa immediately).

Let's do a quick example to illustrate. What follows took me about 5 minutes to find (I cheated a little and used Zen Arbitrage to find this book. You don't need fancy tools to do this. You can do it manually in the Amazon trade-in store.)

Step One: I skimmed books with Amazon trade-in value and looked for books that are selling for "close" to the trade-in amount.

Let's define "close" as within 20%.

I quickly found this book (screenshot from Zen Arbitrage):

| 0133840549 | Applied Statics and Strength of Materials (6th ... | $109.63 | $122.25 | $122.25 | Q | $125.00 |

Here's the book on Amazon:

Applied Statics and Strength of Materials (6th Edition) (Hardcover)
by George F. Limbrunner (Author), et al.

☆☆☆☆☆ ▼ 10 customer reviews   Share 📧 📘 🐦
Access codes and supplements are not guaranteed with used items.

Trade-In Value: $125.

ISBN-13: 978-0133840544
ISBN-10: 0133840549
Why is ISBN important? ▼

Sell yours for a Gift Card
We'll buy it for $125.00
Learn More

Trade in now

Lowest priced used copy: $109.63

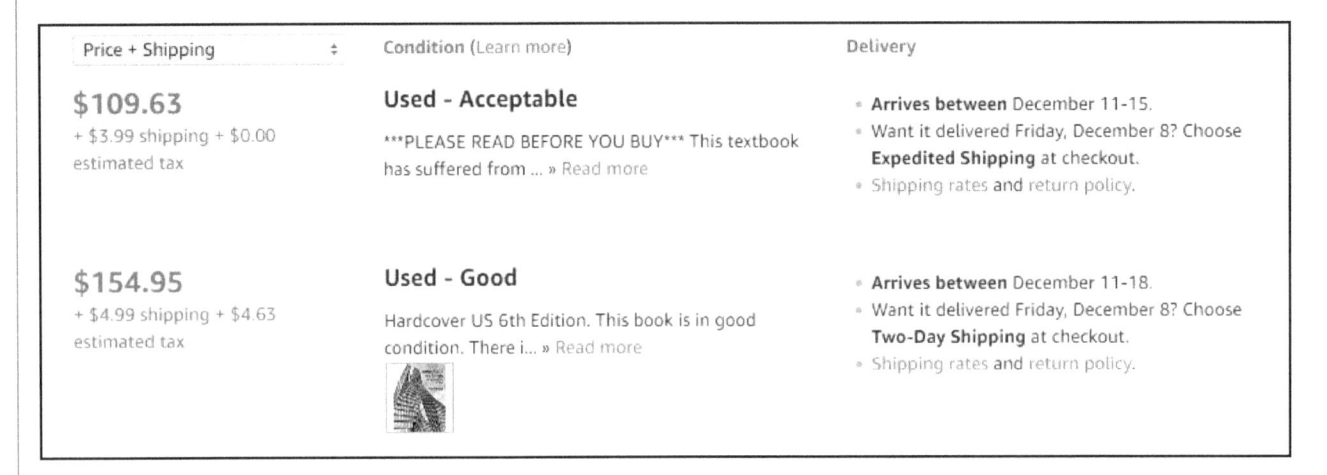

Price + Shipping	Condition (Learn more)	Delivery
$109.63 + $3.99 shipping + $0.00 estimated tax	**Used - Acceptable** ***PLEASE READ BEFORE YOU BUY*** This textbook has suffered from ... » Read more	• **Arrives between** December 11-15. • Want it delivered Friday, December 8? Choose **Expedited Shipping** at checkout. • Shipping rates and return policy.
$154.95 + $4.99 shipping + $4.63 estimated tax	**Used - Good** Hardcover US 6th Edition. This book is in good condition. There i... » Read more	• **Arrives between** December 11-18. • Want it delivered Friday, December 8? Choose **Two-Day Shipping** at checkout. • Shipping rates and return policy.

Yes, this is lower than the trade-in amount, and would be a prime candidate for old-fashioned trade-in credit arbitrage, except the $109 copy is described as having highlighting, and would likely be rejected by Amazon's trade-in criteria. But this is absolutely a book we can sell for cash.

Step Two: I confirmed its price history

Here is the price chart from Keepa:

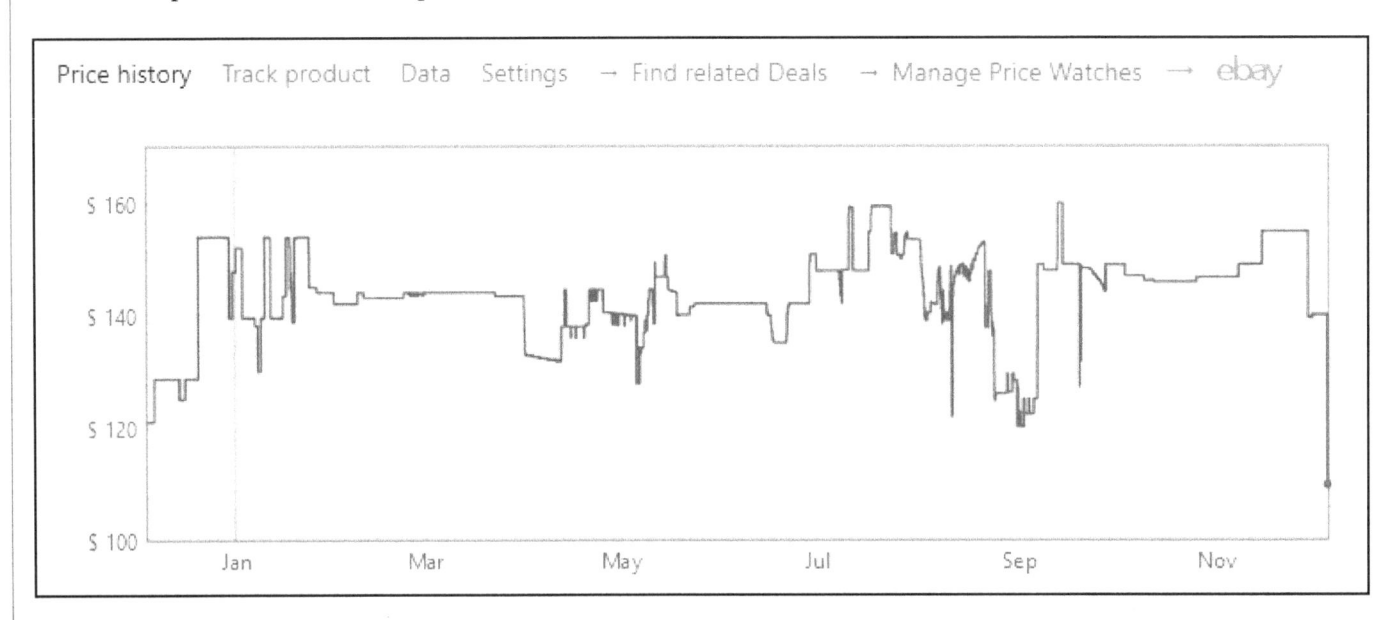

From this 12-month chart, we can confirm this book spends virtually 100% of its time above the price we can currently buy it for, and the vast majority of its time above $130.

Step three: Decide whether to sell Merchant Fulfilled or FBA

I don't sell anything merchant fulfilled, so I already know my answer. But if this were you, you'd have to run the numbers and decide for yourself.

Obvious pros and cons are: MF has lower fees, FBA allows you to sell at a higher price.

(If you're not already an Amazon seller and you're intimidated by this part, I can't stress enough how easy it is to set up an Amazon account. Takes literally two minutes).

Either way, with this book you're making money no matter what. As we're about to see…

So just to cover all our bases, let's examine what our profits would be selling merchant fulfilled, and Fulfillment by Amazon (FBA).

Pricing option #1: Price at the six-month merchant fulfilled average.

Keepa delivers again. We can see the six-month average price for this book is $147.97.

Sales price: $147.97

Net profit: $13.79

Super-low returns here, but again, this is a move for people who want extremely low risk and quick turnover. I would say quickly selling this book for at least $147 is pretty close to a certainty. Not the option I would choose, but I'm just giving you all your options.

Pricing option #2: Price-match the current lowest merchant fulfilled offer.

This would be the most sensible move: Pricing the book at $154.95. The price may go down (or up), but it makes it a strong possibility you'll be among the next few sales (even if the book does have some highlighting).

Sales price: $154.95

Net profit: $19.73

The average rank for the this book is about 260,000, which means this book averages a little less than one sale a day. This should mean a quick sale and quick $20 profit.

Pricing option #3: Match the lowest FBA price.

Sales price: $164.98

Net profit: $20.36

So you see here the FBA fees make the net profit roughly the same. Should still result in a quick sale.

There you go. By utilizing trade-in arbitrage search tactics, I was able to get some quick and low risk cash.

What just happened?

Very quickly, I used trade-in as a baseline figure, then looked for books selling within range of that figure (either a little more or a little less), knowing that anything priced close to the trade-in amount is severely undervalued.

So I used "price proximity" and trade-in arbitrage tactics to find books to sell for cash – skipping trade-in altogether.

The lesson: Amazon trade-in value has two values – one explicit and one implicit

Explicit value: "The amount Amazon will give you in trade-in credit for this item."

Implicit value: "An amount that is significantly below the true market value for this item."

So again, for those who want to skip trade-in and go for cash, the trade-in value still functions as a an anchor price, allowing us to know that any book selling for close to that amount is artificially low and significantly underpriced.

The process, step-by-step

For people who love bullet points, here's the process:

1. Mine Amazon's trade-in store.
2. Find underpriced books (or anything) by looking for a sales price close to the trade-in value.
3. Optional: Search for even cheaper copies using BookFinder.com.
4. Determine the historical average price for the item using Keepa, confirm the book is underpriced.
5. Determine your potential net profits.
6. Buy the book and sell for quick cash.

The takeaway

The tools and tactics of trade-in credit arbitrage is not just for trade-credit – they work for low-risk cash sales too.

The Magic Of "Credit Compounding"

Before we tell you how to turn credit into cash, there's another decision you have to make...

Credit compounding or cash out?

So let's say you follow the step-by-step formula, took $100 in cash and turned it into $120 in Amazon credit. You now have two options:

1. Cash out: Turn that credit into cash as quickly as possible.
2. Credit compounding: "Trade up" to turn $120 into $150, and on and on.

Credit compounding: How it works

You should be able to extrapolate from the name alone how it works. Credit compounding goes like this:

1. Taking a small amount of seed money (say, $100).
2. Finding products online cheaper than their trade-in value, buying them, and trading them in.
3. Then repeating the process and turning that into even more Amazon trade-in credit.

And onwards and onwards, until you're ready to cash out.

How far can you take it? Sky is the limit. Remember that margins are small with Amazon trade-in credit arbitrage, and hunting down opportunity takes time. But the opportunities are out there and there's no limit to how far you can "trade up."

Credit compounding: A simple, conservative math equation

Let's say you steadily receive only 5% returns for your trade-in credit investments. So for every $100 you invest, you get $105 back.

Here's how those numbers work:

- Initial investment: $100
- 1st book: $105
- 10th book: 162.89
- 20th book: 265.33

Again, I went for extremely conservative numbers here, assuming only 5% returns per transaction. Hopefully it will work out a lot for you a lot better than that.

So with 20 trades, you took $100 and turned it into $265 in Amazon credit. It took some time to get there of course, but through the miracle of this kind of "compounded interest," and using some very conservative math, you got there. And to make this extra cool, the risk was slim to none.

Taking this further: A second example, at 10% returns

- Initial investment: $100
- 1st book: $110
- 10th book: 259.37
- 20th book: 672.75

Those numbers are even better. Much better.

So you're ready to cash out

At some point, you're going to decide to stop racking up trade-in credit and cash out. How do you do it?

That's what the next chapter is about...

How To Turn Credit Into Cash (Or Cash Into More Cash)

Now we're going into the fun part: What happens after you've racked up credit? Go on a spending spree for bathrobes, slippers, and pool toys; or turn it into cash?

(That wasn't a trick question. Option #1 is totally legitimate.)

At some point, you're going to decide to stop racking up trade-in credit and cash out. How do you do it?

The answer is in one of three forms of online arbitrage – two I've talked about before this book, and one I haven't.

Credit-to-cash formula #1: Old fashioned "online book arbitrage"

This is the classic "online book arbitrage" formula I've been teaching for over two years. The premise is this:

"Buying cheap 'merchant fulfilled' (non-Prime-eligible) books, and reselling at a higher FBA (Prime-eligible) price."

The step-by-step process for this is simple, but beyond the scope of this book. If you're not familiar with it, I have you covered: This entire online book arbitrage system is covered in the prequel to this book, titled, simply, *Online Book Arbitrage*. (I'm not trying to sell you anything, the book is available for free at www.OnlineBookArbitrage.com. Just cover printing and shipping costs and I'll ship it to you within 2 days.)

It's really worth learning the basic online book arbitrage formula, because of the credit-to-cash methods, this is the most lucrative.

Essentially, you're capitalizing on the price difference between the cheap non-FBA price, and the higher FBA (or "Prime eligible") price. To do this process manually, you simply comb Amazon for books that have this price gap, buy the cheap offer, then ship it into Amazon at the higher FBA price, and profit the difference.

Now that you understand the basic formula, let's continue...

Step #1: Set your online book arbitrage buying criteria

If you're doing trade-in credit arbitrage, we already know you're someone who likes low risk and quick results (in exchange for lower returns), so let's build our criteria around that assumption.

We'll be looking for:

- Textbooks.
- Higher priced ($20+)
- High demand (<100,000 rank)
- Lower ROI: (50%)

With online book arbitrage, it's very easy to find well-ranked books with 50% returns when we're willing to spend $20+ per book.

Step #2: Start compounding the cash

- Start: $100 in trade credit.
- Purchase: Four textbooks.
- Expected returns: 50%
- Turnaround time: 30 days.
- Result: $150 cash.

Now I never tell people to expect all their books to sell within 30 days with online book arbitrage. However in this case, we're focusing on high demand books with low returns. And we're pricing pretty conservatively, so all that should result in fast turnover.

So we just took $100 in Amazon trade credit (or cash, for that matter) and turned it into $150 in cash in 30 days. Consistent 50% returns are virtually unheard of in any investment anywhere (that I'm aware of), so this is pretty amazing in and of itself. But of course, it gets better…

Let's roll our proceeds back into more books.

- Start: $150 in cash.
- Purchase: Six textbooks.
- Expected returns: 50%
- Turnaround time: 30 days.
- Result: $225 cash

Same (simple) online book arbitrage formula. Now we're up to $225 in 60 days. Yes, it won't always work out exactly like this (sometimes better, sometimes worse), but I think this math leans towards conservative.

Let's do this two more times:

- Start: $225 in cash.
- Purchase: Nine textbooks.
- Expected returns: 50%
- Turnaround time: 30 days.
- Result: $340 cash.

And then:

- Start: $340 in cash.
- Purchase: 12 textbooks.
- Expected returns: 50%
- Turnaround time: 30 days.
- Result: $510 cash.

What just happened?

A: We turned $100 in Amazon trade-in credit into $500 in cash in 120 days.

That's not overnight. But getting a 5x return on investment this quickly is almost unheard of in any other investment.

In ancient times you would be burned at the stake for this kind of Merlin-level sorcery. But this isn't magic. This is real and it works.

Credit-to-cash formula #2: The "Underpriced Book Hack" – Selling severely mis-priced books for quick cash

As covered in a previous chapter, the "Underpriced Book Hack" goes like this:

Anytime you can find a book on Amazon that is selling for "close" to the trade-in value, that is a strong indicator that book is significantly underpriced by the seller (probably by accident).

Which means it is a strong indicator that book can be purchased at its cheap price, and immediately resold at its "true market price." And of course, you get to profit the difference.

The premise of this hack is simple: Trade-in value is always less than the true market value of the book. Otherwise, the amount Amazon is offering for a book would be lower.

So to carry out the Underpriced Book Hack, your mission becomes:

- Cruise around Amazon's trade-in store.
- Look for items selling for close to their trade-in amount (say, within 30%)
- Confirm the item is underpriced by reviewing the item's price history in Keepa.
- Buy the underpriced item.
- Sell immediately on Amazon for a cash profit.

By all angles, this is quick, low-risk cash.

Running The Numbers On "The Underpriced Book Hack"

Let's say you take a mere $100 in credit (or cash, doesn't matter). Using the Underpriced Book Hack, with enough hunting, let's say you find enough underpriced books to safely turn that into $150, after all Amazon commissions. Possibly leaning towards optimistic here, but these opportunities are not uncommon.

(Each "round" below represents each time you invest the proceeds into books and convert those books into cash).

Initial investment $100 (credit)

1. 1st round: $150 (cash)
2. 2nd round: $225
3. 3rd round: 337.50
4. 4th round: $506.25
5. 5th round: $759.38

In just 5 cycles (buy, list, sell, repeat), you turned $100 in credit into $759

Again, I think these numbers are pretty reasonable. I'm not getting crazy with unrealistic optimism here. And the only thing this cost you was the time hunting for opportunity on Amazon.

What if we started with $250?

These numbers get crazy, and I don't blame you if you read this in disbelief. But here's how the math works:

Initial investment $250 (credit or cash)

1. 1st round: $375 (cash)
2. 2nd round: $562.50
3. 3rd round: $843.75
4. 4th round: $1,265.63
5. 5th round: $1,898.44

Just for fun, let's do that same math, starting with $500 credit:

Initial investment $500 (credit or cash)

1. 1st round: $750 (cash)
2. 2nd round: $1,125
3. 3rd round: $1,687.50
4. 4th round: $2,531.25
5. 5th round: $3,796.88

That's the miracle of "compounded arbitrage interest."

Credit-to-cash formula #3: Book buyback site arbitrage

This is a great formula for a risk averse" person, because just like Amazon's trade-in program, book buyback programs lock in a price and guarantee it for a set number of days. I don't consider the previous two formulas "risky," but the exact outcome is never certain. With book buy back sites, the outcome *is* certain.

So, you have $100 in Amazon trade-in credit. How do you utilize book buyback sites to "trade up" and walk away with significant cash? By applying the same formula in our step-by-step sample search from a prior chapter. Here's the general outline again:

1. Go to Amazon's trade-in store.
2. Look for books with a higher trade-in value.
3. Run ISBNs through BookFinder or BookScouter, look for the highest cash buy back offer.
4. Run ISBNs through BookFinder.com, and find copies online that are cheaper than the buyback offer.
5. Buy at the low price and sell instantly at the high price.

That's the formula.

And that's how you turn Amazon credit (or cash) into more cash, and on and on until you end up as Scrooge McDuck in a top hat sitting on a giant pile of gold coins.

Using Prep Services To Run A Totally Hands-Off Business

Now we're going to tie everything together into one system that allows you to never have to even touch a book, and have money (or credit) just appear in your account.

Today, it is possible to run an almost entirely outsourced bookselling business - without ever touching a book.

I'm going to break down a simple system for doing exactly that.

What is a prep service?

These are services who accept shipments on your behalf, clean and prep them, and ship them to Amazon for you.

Here's a sample model:

- Purchase the book. Get it shipped to the prep company.
- Share the shipping label with the prep service (via Google docs).
- When the book arrives the prep company verifies the condition of the book and prepares it for shipment.
- They label the items and ship them to Amazon or the book buy back site.

Sounds pretty cool, right?

It is. If you can find a company who will take books for trade-in or buy back sites. Which isn't easy.

First, most prep services won't take books, period. Most will only take new, shrink wrapped items for shipment to an Fulfillment by Amazon warehouse. Used books are considered too much work, there's too much inspection required, and they just won't accept them.

Among the few that will take books, almost none will take books for Amazon's trade-in program or book buy back sites. The same reasons for the aversion applies, only worse: On top of the normal reasons prep services hate books, trade-in books have a high rejection rate by Amazon (because people don't pay attention and order damaged books or the wrong books altogether). This presents an even greater headache for prep services.

I scoured the country for a prep service that would take books and ship them to Amazon's trade-in program or book buy back sites, and only found one who would do it. (Feel free to email me if you want their info.)

With prep services, you are running an entirely virtual business

Now that you never have to touch or even see a book, your only job becomes to scour Amazon for opportunity, order the books, and have money (or credit) simply appear in your bank (or Amazon) account.

Pretty incredible.

Conclusion

That's the formula.

As bonus for taking an interest in this book, I'll be emailing you a bunch of videos covering different aspects of what we've covered so far.

I never wanted to write a book on Amazon trade-in or buy back site arbitrage. But as I covered in the intro, a couple of internet cons and their overpriced program drove me to it. And I'm glad they did. This book is a little bit of karma, giving away for free what they charge $1,000 for. I hope you enjoyed being the beneficiary of this petty (but useful) gesture of revenge.

-Peter Valley

PS: Contact me for any reason at: peter@fbamastery.com

PPS: I give away tons of free material on my website, www.FBAmastery.com. If you're not on my email list already, head over there and get signed up. I have more free ebooks, and lots more.

FBA Mastery
Every trick for selling books and lots more with Fulfillment by Amazon

About the author:

Peter Valley has been selling on Amazon for over 10 years. He is the webmaster of FBAmastery.com, and author of many books and video courses on Amazon selling, including *Book Sourcing Secrets, Amazon Altitude, Pricing Mastery, Condition Hacking*, and more.

He is also the founder of Amazon trade-in arbitrage tool ZenTrade (fbamastery.com/zentrade).

CPSIA information can be obtained
at www.ICGtesting.com
Printed in the USA
BVHW010741031120
592172BV00013B/98